DEDICATION

PREFACE

INTRODUCTION

PART I: UNDERSTANDING AI AND ITS IMPLICATIONS

CHAPTER 1: AI FUNDAMENTALS

CHAPTER 2: THE AI-DRIVEN TRANSFORMATION

CHAPTER 3: ETHICAL AND SOCIAL CONSIDERATIONS

PART II: LEADERSHIP IN THE AI ERA

CHAPTER 4: REDEFINING LEADERSHIP

CHAPTER 5: LEADING WITH AI

CHAPTER 6: BUILDING AI-POWERED ORGANIZATIONS

PART III: LEADERSHIP COMPETENCIES FOR THE AI ERA

CHAPTER 7: STRATEGIC THINKING AND VISION

CHAPTER 8: COLLABORATION AND TEAMWORK

CHAPTER 9: COMMUNICATION AND INFLUENCE

CHAPTER 10: ADAPTABILITY AND RESILIENCE

PART IV: PERSPECTIVES ON AI AND LEADERSHIP

CHAPTER 11: ENHANCEMENT PERSPECTIVE

CHAPTER 12: REPLACEMENT PERSPECTIVE

CHAPTER 13: SKEPTICAL PERSPECTIVE

CONCLUSION

Thank you for picking up my book. Your support means a lot, and I hope you find the read both enjoyable and insightful. Beyond being an author, my work extends into research and consultancy within organizational behavior and leadership. I engage with a broad spectrum of clients, from individuals to larger teams and organizations, offering guidance in leadership development.

For a deeper dive into my professional background and consulting philosophy, several websites are available. There, you'll also find my contact details. I'm eager to hear your thoughts on the book or discuss potential collaboration in leadership coaching.

Discover more about my work and other publications related to leadership and organizational behavior at my personal website, https://thomaspatrickhuber.com.

Learn about my specific approach to leadership coaching and consulting at https://elevateus.ch, the official website of my company.

Lastly, in case you want to reach out to me directly please send me an email at thomaspatrick@mac.com. I appreciate your support in purchasing this book and look forward to connecting with you.

Wishing you an enlightening journey,

Thomas P Huber, PhD, MS ECS

Dedication

To all those who worry about the rise of artificial intelligence, may this book provide clarity and reassurance in understanding its profound potential and manageable risks.

To the AI enthusiasts driving innovation, your vision and curiosity inspire us to explore new frontiers and redefine the possibilities of our future.

And to everyone sitting on the sidelines, may this journey into the world of AI ignite your curiosity and empower you to engage with the technological revolution shaping our world.

This book is for you—let's lead the future together.

Preface

In recent years, artificial intelligence has emerged as a transformative force, reshaping industries, economies, and societies at an unprecedented pace. From automating routine tasks to providing sophisticated data-driven insights, AI is redefining the way we work, live, and lead. As we stand on the brink of this technological revolution, it is crucial to understand not only the capabilities and implications of AI but also how it will influence and reshape the fundamental principles of leadership.

"Leading the Future: Mastering Leadership in the AI Revolution" was born out of a desire to explore the intersection of AI and leadership. This book aims to equip leaders, managers, and aspiring professionals with the knowledge and tools needed to navigate the complexities of the AI era. Whether you are an AI enthusiast, a skeptic, or someone who is still undecided, this book will provide you with a comprehensive understanding of AI's impact on leadership and how to harness its potential for your organization.

Throughout the pages of this book, we research the fundamentals of AI, examining its various types and technologies, and exploring its transformative effects on business models and operations. We also address the ethical and social considerations that accompany AI's rise, highlighting the importance of fairness, privacy, and societal values in the development and deployment of AI systems.

In the second part of the book, we focus on the evolving landscape of leadership in the AI era. Traditional leadership models are being challenged, and there is a growing need for leaders who are adaptive, agile, and innovative. We explore how AI can be integrated into leadership strategies, enhancing decision-making processes and fostering AI-powered organizations. We also discuss the essential competencies that leaders must develop to thrive in this new environment, from strategic thinking and collaboration to effective communication and resilience.

One of the unique aspects of this book is our exploration of three key perspectives on AI and leadership: the enhancement perspective, which views AI as a valuable assistant to current leadership functions; the replacement perspective, which considers the potential for AI to take on more significant leadership roles; and the skeptical perspective, which critically examines the limitations and oversold promises of AI. By presenting these diverse viewpoints, we aim to provide a balanced and nuanced understanding of AI's role in leadership.

As you embark on this journey, we invite you to engage with the ideas presented in this book with an open mind and a critical eye. The future of leadership in the AI era is not set in stone; it is being shaped by our collective actions, decisions, and innovations. Together, we can navigate the challenges and seize the opportunities that AI presents, leading our organizations and societies toward a brighter, more inclusive future.

Thank you for joining us on this exploration of leadership in the age of AI. We hope that this book inspires you, informs you, and empowers you to lead with confidence and vision in the face of rapid technological change.

Sincerely,

Thomas P Huber PhD, MS ECS

Introduction

Artificial Intelligence (AI) has rapidly transitioned from a futuristic concept to a transformative force shaping the world today. Its evolution, driven by advancements in machine learning, natural language processing, and neural networks, has led to its integration into a wide array of industries, fundamentally altering how businesses operate and compete.

In healthcare, AI systems are revolutionizing diagnostics, treatment planning, and patient care. AI algorithms can analyze medical images with remarkable accuracy, often detecting conditions that escape the human eye. Predictive analytics, powered by AI, are enabling personalized medicine, tailoring treatments to individual patients based on genetic and historical data. This not only enhances patient outcomes but also optimizes operational efficiency within healthcare systems. The financial sector, too, has seen significant disruption due to AI. Automated trading systems, driven by complex algorithms, execute trades at speeds and efficiencies unattainable by human traders. AI-powered risk management tools assess and predict market risks, helping institutions safeguard against potential financial crises. Moreover, customer service within banks and financial institutions has been enhanced by AI-driven chatbots and virtual assistants, providing 24/7 support and personalized financial advice.

In the realm of manufacturing, AI is at the core of the Industry 4.0 revolution. Smart factories equipped with AI-powered robots and automation systems are streamlining production processes, reducing errors, and increasing efficiency. Predictive maintenance, another AI application, allows manufacturers to foresee equipment failures before they occur, thereby minimizing downtime and maintenance costs. This leads to a more resilient and responsive manufacturing sector, capable of meeting the dynamic demands of the global market.

The retail industry is leveraging AI to redefine customer experiences and optimize operations. AI-driven recommendation engines analyze consumer behavior to provide personalized shopping experiences, boosting customer satisfaction and sales. Inventory management systems, enhanced by AI, predict stock requirements, reducing both overstock and stockouts. Additionally, AI-powered chatbots and virtual shopping assistants offer customers immediate support and personalized assistance, transforming the retail landscape into a more interactive and customer-centric environment.

Transportation and logistics have also been profoundly impacted by AI. Autonomous vehicles, once a staple of science fiction, are now a reality, promising to revolutionize personal and commercial transportation. AI algorithms optimize route planning and logistics, reducing fuel consumption, delivery times, and operational costs. In aviation, AI assists in air traffic management, enhancing safety and efficiency in increasingly crowded skies. The creative industries are not immune to AI's influence. In media and entertainment, AI algorithms curate content, predict viewer preferences, and even generate music and scripts. The gaming industry employs AI to create more realistic and responsive non-player characters, enhancing the gaming experience. In advertising, AI-driven analytics enable hyper-targeted marketing campaigns, delivering the right message to the right audience at the right time.

As AI continues to advance, its impact on industries will only grow more profound. The integration of AI into business operations is not just a technological upgrade but a strategic imperative. Organizations that harness the power of AI can achieve unprecedented levels of efficiency, innovation, and competitiveness. However, this rapid transformation also brings challenges and uncertainties that leaders must navigate to ensure sustainable and ethical AI implementation.

In the following sections of this book, we will go deeper into the implications of AI for leadership, exploring how leaders can adapt to and thrive in this AI-driven world. We will examine the fundamental shifts in leadership paradigms, the integration of AI into decision-making processes, and the development of essential competencies for leading in the AI era. Through this exploration, we aim to provide a comprehensive guide for current and future leaders, equipping them with the insights and tools necessary to lead with confidence and vision in the age of AI. Beyond its impact on industries, AI is increasingly transforming our personal lives and homes. Smart home devices, powered by AI, are becoming integral parts of our daily routines. Voice-activated assistants like Amazon's Alexa, Google Assistant, and Apple's Siri manage our schedules, control smart home appliances, and provide instant access to information. These AI assistants learn from our preferences and behaviors, offering a more personalized and convenient living experience.

AI-driven home security systems offer enhanced safety through advanced surveillance, facial recognition, and anomaly detection. These systems can alert homeowners of potential threats in real-time, providing peace of mind and a higher level of protection.

In the realm of entertainment, AI-powered streaming services like Netflix and Spotify recommend content tailored to individual tastes, making it easier to discover new shows, movies, and music that align with our preferences. AI algorithms analyze viewing and listening habits to curate personalized content, enhancing our entertainment experiences. AI is also revolutionizing personal health and fitness. Wearable devices equipped with AI track physical activity, monitor vital signs, and provide insights into overall health. Personalized fitness plans and virtual coaching powered by AI help individuals achieve their health and wellness goals more effectively.

AI's influence extends to our interactions and relationships. Social media platforms use AI to curate feeds, recommend connections, and moderate content, shaping how we communicate and engage with the world. AI-driven language translation tools break down language barriers, enabling seamless communication across different languages and cultures.

Leaders today must navigate the complexities of AI implementation, ensuring that their organizations harness the benefits of AI while mitigating its risks. This requires a deep understanding of AI technologies, their capabilities, and their limitations. Leaders must be adept at integrating AI into their strategic vision, fostering a culture of innovation and agility, and making informed decisions based on data-driven insights.

One of the key challenges for leaders is balancing the technological capabilities of AI with the human elements of leadership. While AI can enhance decision-making, improve efficiency, and drive innovation, it cannot replace the empathy, creativity, and ethical judgment that human leaders bring. Effective leaders must therefore find ways to leverage AI as a tool that complements and enhances human capabilities rather than replacing them.

The ethical implications of AI use demand vigilant leadership. Issues such as bias in AI algorithms, data privacy, and the societal impact of AI-driven decisions require leaders to adopt a principled approach to AI governance. Leaders must ensure that AI systems are designed and used in ways that are fair, transparent, and aligned with the organization's values and societal norms. The AI era also calls for leaders who are adaptable and resilient. The pace of technological change means that leaders must be prepared to continually learn and evolve. This involves not only keeping abreast of technological advancements but also fostering a culture of continuous improvement and learning within their organizations.

Effective leadership in the AI era also involves fostering collaboration between human employees and AI systems. Leaders must create environments where AI and human capabilities complement each other, driving innovation and efficiency. This requires a deep understanding of both human and machine strengths and the ability to integrate them seamlessly into organizational workflows.

Leaders must be proactive in addressing the workforce implications of AI. As AI automates certain tasks, there is a growing need for reskilling and upskilling employees to ensure they remain relevant in the changing job landscape. Leaders must invest in training and development programs that equip employees with the skills needed to work alongside AI systems.

In this book, we will explore how leaders can rise to these challenges and thrive in the AI era. We will investigate the evolving landscape of leadership, examining how traditional leadership models are being reshaped by AI, and what new competencies are required for leaders to succeed. Through practical insights and real-world examples, we aim to provide a comprehensive guide for leaders who are navigating the complex and rapidly changing world of AI.

Join us on this journey as we uncover the strategies and skills needed to lead effectively in the age of AI, ensuring that we harness the power of this transformative technology to create a better, more equitable, and innovative future.

This book is designed to be a comprehensive guide for a diverse audience, spanning across different roles and industries. Whether you are a seasoned executive, a mid-level manager, an aspiring leader, or simply someone interested in the transformative potential of AI, this book has been crafted with you in mind.

For those at the helm of organizations, we offer strategic insights into how AI can be leveraged to drive innovation, efficiency, and competitive advantage. It delves into the integration of AI within business strategies, the ethical considerations of AI deployment, and the cultivation of a forward-thinking, AI-ready organizational culture. Senior executives will find guidance on how to lead their organizations through the complexities of AI implementation and transformation.

Mid-level managers and team leaders play a crucial role in bridging the gap between senior leadership and the broader workforce. This book provides practical advice on how to implement AI technologies at the operational level, foster collaboration between human teams and AI systems, and manage the change that AI brings to everyday workflows. It also highlights the importance of continuous learning and adaptability, key traits for leaders at this level.

For those new to leadership or aspiring to take on leadership roles, this book serves as a foundational resource. It covers the basics of AI technologies, their potential applications, and the evolving leadership competencies needed in the AI era. Aspiring leaders will gain an understanding of how to harness AI to make data-driven decisions, innovate, and drive organizational success.

HR and talent development professionals are integral to preparing the workforce for the AI-driven future. This book offers insights into attracting, developing, and retaining AI talent, as well as strategies for reskilling and upskilling employees. It addresses the need for creating a supportive culture that encourages learning and adaptation, ensuring that the human workforce can thrive alongside AI.

For AI enthusiasts and technologists, this book provides a broader perspective on how AI intersects with leadership and organizational strategy. It goes beyond the technical aspects of AI, exploring its implications for business, society, and human interaction. Technologists will find value in understanding the leadership challenges and opportunities that accompany AI adoption. Educators and students in fields such as business, technology, and leadership studies will find this book a valuable addition to their curriculum. It synthesizes current research, real-world examples, and practical advice, making it a useful resource for teaching and learning about the intersection of AI and leadership.

For the general reader with an interest in AI and leadership, we offer an accessible and engaging exploration of these topics. It demystifies AI, explains its impact on leadership, and provides a roadmap for navigating the AI-driven future. "Leading the Future: Mastering Leadership in the AI Revolution" is aimed at anyone who seeks to understand the profound changes AI brings and how to lead effectively in this new era. Through this book, we hope to equip you with the knowledge, insights, and tools needed to harness the power of AI and become a leader who can navigate the complexities of our rapidly evolving world.

We have structured the book to provide a comprehensive understanding of AI's impact on leadership and to equip readers with the knowledge and skills needed to thrive in the AI era. It is divided into three main parts, each focusing on a critical aspect of AI and leadership.

The first part lays the foundation by exploring the fundamentals of AI. It begins with a detailed explanation of what AI is, including its various types such as narrow AI, general AI, and superintelligent AI. It then dives into key AI technologies like machine learning, deep learning, and natural language processing, examining their current and potential applications across different industries. This part also addresses the profound transformations AI is driving in business models, processes, and operations, highlighting both the opportunities and challenges it presents. Furthermore, it discusses the ethical and social considerations of AI, including concerns about bias, privacy, and the broader impact on societal values and norms.

The second part of the book focuses on how leadership needs to evolve in response to the AI revolution. It begins by redefining traditional leadership models, emphasizing the need for adaptive, agile, and innovative leadership styles that can thrive in a rapidly changing environment. This section covers how leaders can integrate AI into their strategies and decision-making processes, leveraging AI for data-driven insights and optimal performance. It explores the importance of balancing human and AI capabilities and provides guidance on fostering an AI-ready culture within organizations. This part also addresses the practical aspects of building AI-powered organizations, from attracting and developing AI talent to implementing effective AI governance and risk management frameworks.

In the final section, the book focuses on the specific competencies leaders need to develop to succeed in the AI era. It starts with strategic thinking and vision, discussing how leaders can anticipate and navigate AI-driven disruptions and develop AI-enabled business strategies. It then moves on to collaboration and teamwork, emphasizing the importance of building cross-functional and interdisciplinary teams, facilitating human-AI collaboration, and promoting trust and transparency in AI systems. Communication and influence are also key themes, with practical advice on how to effectively communicate AI-related initiatives, influence stakeholders, and build AI literacy across the organization. Finally, it explores adaptability and resilience, highlighting the need for leaders to embrace change, develop resilience, and foster a culture of continuous learning and improvement.

Several key themes run throughout the book, providing a cohesive narrative that ties together the various chapters and sections. These include the transformative power of AI and how it is reshaping industries, businesses, and personal lives; the importance of integrating AI in ways that complement and enhance human capabilities; the need for principled approaches to AI governance, addressing issues of bias, privacy, and societal impact; the critical importance of fostering a culture of learning and agility to keep pace with rapid technological changes; and practical guidance on how to incorporate AI into business strategies and operations effectively.

By exploring these themes in depth, "Leading the Future: Mastering Leadership in the AI Revolution" aims to provide a comprehensive roadmap for leaders who are navigating the complexities and opportunities of the AI era.

Part I: Understanding AI and Its Implications

In this first part of the book, we build a strong foundation of knowledge about AI and its far-reaching implications. Understanding how AI is transforming our world is crucial for grasping what it means for leadership in the AI era.

We begin with an exploration of AI fundamentals. Imagine a world where machines not only perform specific tasks but also exhibit broader capabilities akin to human intelligence. This is the realm of AI, which comes in various types: narrow AI, general AI, and the even more advanced superintelligent AI. Narrow AI is designed for specific tasks, while general AI has broader capabilities similar to human intelligence. Superintelligent AI surpasses human cognitive abilities, envisioning a future where machines exceed our own mental capacities. In this chapter, we delve into key AI technologies such as machine learning, deep learning, and natural language processing, explaining how they work and their significance. We also examine the current and potential applications of AI across different sectors, showcasing its versatility and transformative power in industries and daily life.

Next, we explore AI's profound impact on business models, processes, and operations. AI is not just a technological innovation; it is reshaping traditional business frameworks, introducing new efficiencies, and creating innovative opportunities. This chapter addresses the various challenges presented by AI, such as integrating new technologies, adapting the workforce, and navigating ethical considerations. The changing nature of work and the workforce is another key focus, highlighting how AI is redefining job roles, skill requirements, and organizational structures.

We then turn our attention to the ethical and social considerations of AI. Critical issues such as AI bias and fairness come to the forefront, exploring how biases can be introduced into AI systems and their impact on society. Privacy and security implications are also crucial, emphasizing the importance of safeguarding personal data and ensuring the security of AI systems. Moreover, we consider the broader role of AI in shaping societal values and norms, addressing how AI can influence and potentially transform cultural and ethical landscapes.

By the end of this section, you will have a solid understanding of the fundamental concepts of AI, the transformative effects of AI on businesses and society, and the critical ethical and social issues that must be addressed. This knowledge will provide a strong foundation for exploring how leadership must adapt and evolve in response to AI's growing influence.

Chapter 1: AI Fundamentals

The journey into the AI era begins with understanding the essence of artificial intelligence itself. AI, once a staple of science fiction, has become an integral part of our reality, driving significant advancements and changes across various domains. The AI revolution is characterized by its ability to replicate and even surpass certain aspects of human intelligence, fundamentally altering how we interact with technology and the world around us.

At the heart of AI lies its capacity to process vast amounts of data and learn from it. This is where machine learning comes into play, a subset of AI that enables systems to improve their performance based on experience. Machine learning algorithms analyze patterns within data, make predictions, and refine their outputs without being explicitly programmed for each task. This ability to learn and adapt makes AI a powerful tool for tackling complex problems and automating tasks that were once thought to require human intelligence.

Deep learning, another critical aspect of AI, takes this capability further. Inspired by the human brain's neural networks, deep learning involves layers of algorithms that process data in a hierarchical manner. This approach allows AI systems to understand intricate patterns and make sense of unstructured data such as images, speech, and text. Deep learning has been instrumental in breakthroughs like advanced image recognition, natural language processing, and autonomous driving.

Natural language processing (NLP) is yet another transformative technology within the AI landscape. NLP enables machines to understand, interpret, and generate human language. From chatbots providing customer support to complex systems translating languages in real-time, NLP is revolutionizing communication and information retrieval. It is the driving force behind virtual assistants like Siri, Alexa, and Google Assistant, making human-computer interactions more intuitive and seamless.

The applications of AI span a wide array of industries. In healthcare, AI aids in diagnosing diseases, predicting patient outcomes, and personalizing treatment plans. Financial institutions use AI to detect fraudulent activities, automate trading, and provide personalized financial advice. In manufacturing, AI optimizes supply chains, predicts maintenance needs, and enhances quality control. Retailers leverage AI to personalize shopping experiences, manage inventory, and streamline logistics. These examples only scratch the surface of AI's potential, highlighting its transformative impact across sectors.

The AI revolution is not without its challenges. Integrating AI into existing systems and workflows can be complex and resource-intensive. There are also concerns about the displacement of jobs as AI automates tasks traditionally performed by humans. Ethical considerations, such as ensuring fairness and transparency in AI decision-making, safeguarding privacy, and preventing misuse, are critical issues that must be addressed as AI continues to evolve.

As we navigate through the complexities and opportunities of AI, it is essential to understand the different types of AI. Narrow AI, also known as weak AI, is designed to perform specific tasks. It excels in areas such as speech recognition, image classification, and recommendation systems but lacks general cognitive abilities. General AI, or strong AI, possesses the ability to understand, learn, and apply knowledge across a wide range of tasks, much like a human. While general AI remains largely theoretical, advancements in this field are steadily progressing. Superintelligent AI goes beyond human intelligence, performing tasks that are currently unimaginable. The ethical implications and potential risks associated with superintelligent AI are subjects of ongoing debate and research.

Understanding these foundational aspects of AI—its technologies, applications, and types—is crucial for grasping the broader implications of the AI revolution. As we delve deeper into the book, we will explore how these technological advancements are reshaping industries, transforming business models, and influencing societal norms and values. This knowledge sets the stage for examining how leadership must adapt and evolve in the face of rapid technological change, ensuring that we harness the power of AI to create a better future for all.

Key AI technologies encompass several critical areas that drive the functionality and advancements in artificial intelligence. Machine learning is at the core of AI, involving algorithms that enable systems to learn from data and improve over time without being explicitly programmed. The primary types of machine learning are supervised, unsupervised, and reinforcement learning. In supervised learning, models are trained on labeled data, allowing them to predict outcomes based on input-output pairs. Unsupervised learning deals with unlabeled data, where the system tries to identify patterns and structures. Reinforcement learning involves training models to make sequences of decisions by rewarding desirable behaviors and penalizing undesirable ones. Examples of machine learning applications include spam detection, recommendation systems, and predictive maintenance.

Deep learning, a subset of machine learning, is characterized by its use of neural networks with multiple layers. Unlike traditional machine learning, which often relies on shallow networks, deep learning utilizes deep neural networks that can model complex patterns in data. Neural networks function by processing inputs through interconnected layers of nodes or neurons, each layer transforming the data in increasingly abstract ways. Key breakthroughs in deep learning include the development of convolutional neural networks (CNNs) for image processing and recurrent neural networks (RNNs) for sequential data. These advancements have led to significant improvements in areas such as image and speech recognition, natural language processing, and autonomous driving.

Natural Language Processing (NLP) focuses on the interaction between computers and human language. It involves the ability of machines to understand, interpret, and generate human language in a way that is both meaningful and useful. NLP encompasses tasks such as text generation, sentiment analysis, and translation. Text generation involves creating coherent and contextually relevant text based on given inputs. Sentiment analysis determines the sentiment expressed in a piece of text, which can be positive, negative, or neutral. Translation refers to converting text from one language to another while preserving its meaning. Real-world applications of NLP include virtual assistants like Siri and Alexa, chatbots for customer service, and automated translation services.

Computer vision is another critical area of AI, enabling machines to interpret and make decisions based on visual data. It involves image recognition, object detection, and facial recognition. Image recognition is the process of identifying objects, places, or people in images. Object detection goes a step further by not only recognizing objects but also determining their locations within an image. Facial recognition identifies and verifies individuals based on their facial features. Applications of computer vision span various industries, from healthcare, where it aids in medical imaging and diagnostics, to security, where it is used for surveillance and access control, and retail, where it enhances customer experience through automated checkouts and personalized shopping.

These key AI technologies form the backbone of modern AI systems, driving advancements across multiple domains and enabling the development of intelligent applications that are transforming industries and everyday life. Current applications of AI are diverse and impactful across various sectors. In healthcare, AI is revolutionizing diagnostics and personalized medicine. Machine learning algorithms analyze medical images, aiding in the detection of diseases such as cancer and diabetic retinopathy with greater accuracy and speed than human experts. Personalized medicine benefits from AI's ability to process genetic information and patient data to recommend tailored treatment plans, improving outcomes and reducing adverse effects. Predictive analytics in patient management helps in anticipating health issues before they become critical, enabling proactive interventions and better resource allocation.

In finance, AI enhances fraud detection and risk management. AI systems monitor transactions in real time, identifying unusual patterns that could indicate fraudulent activity. This continuous surveillance and immediate response capability surpass traditional methods, protecting both institutions and customers from financial crimes. Automated trading leverages AI algorithms to analyze market trends and execute trades at optimal times, maximizing profits. Financial planning is also improved through AI-driven advisory services that provide personalized investment strategies based on individual risk profiles and financial goals.

Retail is another sector where AI is making significant strides. Personalized recommendations enhance the shopping experience by analyzing customer behavior and preferences to suggest products that align with their tastes. This increases customer satisfaction and drives sales. AI-powered customer service through chatbots and virtual assistants provides instant support, handling inquiries, processing orders, and resolving issues efficiently. Inventory management and logistics benefit from AI's predictive capabilities, ensuring optimal stock levels, reducing waste, and improving supply chain efficiency.

Transportation is experiencing transformative changes due to AI, particularly in the development of autonomous vehicles. Self-driving cars utilize AI to navigate complex environments, make split-second decisions, and avoid obstacles, aiming to reduce accidents and improve traffic flow. Traffic management systems use AI to analyze real-time traffic data, optimizing signal timings and reducing congestion. Predictive maintenance for vehicles and infrastructure ensures timely repairs and replacements, minimizing downtime and extending the lifespan of assets. Logistics optimization powered by AI streamlines routing and scheduling, enhancing delivery efficiency and reducing costs.

Challenges and limitations of AI encompass a range of technical, ethical, and social issues that must be addressed to fully realize its potential. Technical challenges are prominent, particularly concerning data quality and availability. AI systems rely heavily on large datasets to function accurately and effectively. Poor-quality data, which may be incomplete, outdated, or biased, can lead to flawed outcomes. Ensuring data is clean, comprehensive, and representative remains a significant hurdle. Additionally, the availability of data varies across sectors and geographies, impacting the development and application of AI in certain areas.

Algorithmic limitations and computational power present further technical challenges. While AI algorithms have advanced significantly, they are not infallible and can struggle with tasks requiring deep understanding or contextual awareness. Developing algorithms that can generalize well across different scenarios without extensive retraining is an ongoing challenge. Furthermore, AI systems often require substantial computational resources, which can be expensive and energy-intensive. Balancing the need for powerful computing capabilities with cost and sustainability considerations is a critical issue.

Ethical and social challenges also play a crucial role in the deployment and acceptance of AI. Bias and fairness in AI systems are major concerns, as AI can perpetuate or even exacerbate existing biases present in training data. This can lead to unfair treatment and discrimination in applications such as hiring, lending, and law enforcement. Ensuring that AI systems are fair and unbiased requires careful design, rigorous testing, and continuous monitoring.

Privacy concerns and data security are paramount as AI systems often process sensitive personal information. Safeguarding this data against breaches and unauthorized access is essential to maintain trust and comply with regulations like GDPR and CCPA. The use of AI in surveillance and data collection also raises questions about the balance between security and individual privacy rights.

The impact of AI on employment and the workforce is another significant social challenge. While AI can create new opportunities and roles, it also poses a risk of job displacement, particularly for tasks that can be automated. This transition can lead to economic inequality and social unrest if not managed carefully. Reskilling and upskilling programs are essential to prepare the workforce for the changing job landscape and to ensure that workers can transition to new roles that leverage AI technologies.

Future directions in AI encompass a range of emerging technologies, potential breakthroughs, and a long-term vision for AI's role in society. As AI continues to evolve, several emerging technologies and research areas are poised to shape its future. One such area is explainable AI, which aims to make AI systems more transparent and understandable to humans. This addresses the "black box" problem, where AI's decision-making processes are opaque. By improving interpretability, explainable AI can build trust and facilitate better human-AI collaboration.

Another promising area is edge AI, which involves deploying AI algorithms on local devices rather than centralized servers. This approach reduces latency, enhances privacy, and lowers bandwidth usage, making AI applications more efficient and responsive. Edge AI is particularly relevant for Internet of Things (IoT) devices, autonomous vehicles, and real-time analytics.

Potential breakthroughs and innovations in AI are expected to drive significant advancements across various fields. One such breakthrough is in the development of more advanced natural language processing (NLP) models. These models will enable AI systems to understand and generate human language with greater accuracy and nuance, improving applications in customer service, content creation, and translation.

In the realm of healthcare, AI-driven innovations like personalized medicine and advanced diagnostic tools promise to revolutionize patient care. By analyzing genetic information, medical histories, and real-time health data, AI can provide tailored treatment plans and early detection of diseases, significantly improving patient outcomes.

Quantum computing represents another frontier with the potential to transform AI. Quantum computers can process information at unprecedented speeds, enabling AI algorithms to solve complex problems that are currently infeasible for classical computers. This could lead to breakthroughs in cryptography, material science, and drug discovery.

The long-term vision for AI and its role in society involves a harmonious integration of AI technologies into daily life, enhancing human capabilities and addressing global challenges. AI has the potential to drive economic growth, improve quality of life, and promote sustainability. For instance, AI can optimize energy usage, reduce waste, and support environmental conservation efforts, contributing to a more sustainable future.

In education, AI can provide personalized learning experiences, helping students achieve their full potential by tailoring educational content to their individual needs and learning styles. This can democratize access to high-quality education and bridge gaps in educational attainment. AI's role in addressing global health issues is also significant. AI-powered tools can enhance disease surveillance, track outbreaks, and assist in developing vaccines and treatments. By enabling rapid response and informed decision-making, AI can play a crucial role in managing and mitigating global health crises.

Realizing this long-term vision requires addressing ethical, legal, and societal challenges. Ensuring that AI systems are developed and deployed responsibly is paramount. This includes safeguarding privacy, preventing bias, and ensuring that AI benefits are distributed equitably. Collaborative efforts among governments, industry, academia, and civil society will be essential to establish frameworks that promote ethical AI development and use.

The future of AI is bright, with numerous emerging technologies and potential breakthroughs on the horizon. As AI continues to evolve, its integration into various aspects of society promises to enhance human capabilities and address pressing global challenges. By fostering innovation, ensuring ethical practices, and promoting collaboration, we can harness the full potential of AI for the betterment of society.

The importance of understanding AI's potential lies in its ability to transform industries by enhancing efficiency, accuracy, and decision-making capabilities. For instance, AI can process vast amounts of data rapidly, providing valuable insights that would be impossible for humans to achieve manually. It has applications across various fields, from healthcare and finance to retail and transportation, each benefiting from AI's ability to optimize processes, predict trends, and personalize services.

However, it is equally important to be aware of AI's limitations. AI systems are heavily dependent on data quality and availability. Poor or biased data can lead to flawed outcomes, and AI's current capabilities are limited in tasks requiring emotional intelligence, creativity, and ethical judgment. Additionally, AI's impact on employment, privacy, and ethical considerations cannot be overlooked. Addressing these challenges requires robust governance frameworks, ethical guidelines, and continuous monitoring.

The role of continuous learning and adaptation in the AI era is paramount. As AI technologies advance rapidly, staying informed about the latest developments is essential for leaders and organizations. Continuous learning ensures that individuals and teams can effectively leverage new AI tools and techniques. Adapting to the evolving AI landscape also involves fostering a culture of innovation, where experimentation and risk-taking are encouraged. This approach enables organizations to remain agile and competitive in a dynamic environment.

Leaders must balance the analytical power of AI with human qualities such as empathy, creativity, and ethical reasoning. By integrating AI with these human traits, leaders can enhance their decision-making processes while maintaining the human touch essential for building trust and fostering strong relationships within their teams.

The integration of AI into various sectors offers tremendous opportunities for innovation and growth. Understanding AI fundamentals, recognizing its potential and limitations, and committing to continuous learning and adaptation are critical for harnessing AI's full potential. As we navigate the complexities of the AI era, a balanced approach that combines AI's capabilities with human intelligence will be key to achieving sustainable success and positive societal impact.

Chapter 2: The AI-Driven Transformation

The AI-driven transformation in leadership marks a significant shift in how leaders operate and make decisions. Artificial Intelligence (AI) has begun to fundamentally alter the landscape of leadership by introducing new tools and capabilities that enhance efficiency, decision-making, and strategic planning. This transformation is characterized by the integration of advanced data analytics, machine learning, and automation into everyday business processes. Leaders now have access to unprecedented amounts of data and insights, enabling them to make more informed and timely decisions. AI-driven tools can analyze vast datasets to identify patterns, predict trends, and provide actionable recommendations, thus optimizing business operations and driving innovation.

The imperative for leaders to adapt in the AI era is clear. The rapid pace of technological advancement means that organizations must remain agile and responsive to stay competitive. Leaders who fail to embrace AI risk falling behind as their competitors leverage these technologies to gain a strategic advantage. Adaptation involves more than just adopting new tools; it requires a fundamental shift in mindset and leadership style. Leaders must be willing to embrace continuous learning, staying updated on the latest AI developments and understanding how to integrate these technologies effectively into their organizations.

The role of a leader is evolving from one of directive decision-making to one that emphasizes collaboration between human intelligence and AI. Leaders must cultivate a culture that encourages innovation, experimentation, and the responsible use of AI. This includes addressing ethical considerations, such as data privacy, bias, and the broader social implications of AI deployment. Leaders must ensure that AI systems are designed and used in ways that are fair, transparent, and aligned with the organization's values.

The adaptation process also involves reskilling and upskilling the workforce. As AI automates routine tasks, leaders must help their teams develop new skills that complement AI capabilities. This not only ensures that employees remain relevant and valuable but also fosters a culture of growth and resilience within the organization. By investing in employee development and creating pathways for continuous learning, leaders can build a workforce that is adaptable and capable of leveraging AI to its fullest potential.

Changes in traditional business models due to AI integration are significant. AI allows businesses to shift from reactive to proactive strategies by using predictive analytics to anticipate market trends and customer needs. This shift leads to more dynamic and adaptable business models that can respond swiftly to changing conditions. For example, subscription-based models and personalized services have become more prevalent, driven by AI's ability to analyze consumer data and predict preferences. This has led to more customer-centric approaches, where products and services are tailored to individual needs and delivered with greater efficiency.

AI's role in optimizing processes and enhancing operational efficiency is transformative. By automating routine and repetitive tasks, AI frees up human resources to focus on more strategic and creative activities. In manufacturing, AI-driven automation can streamline production lines, reducing errors and increasing output. In supply chain management, AI algorithms optimize routing and inventory levels, minimizing costs and improving delivery times. AI also enhances decision-making processes by providing real-time insights and recommendations based on large datasets, leading to more informed and effective business strategies.

Examples of AI-driven transformations in various industries illustrate the broad impact of these technologies. In healthcare, AI is revolutionizing diagnostics and personalized medicine. AI systems analyze medical images and patient data to detect diseases early and recommend tailored treatment plans, improving patient outcomes and operational efficiency. In finance, AI is used for fraud detection and risk management, where it identifies unusual patterns in transactions and provides alerts in real-time. Automated trading platforms use AI to execute trades at optimal times, maximizing returns and minimizing risks.

The retail industry has seen significant AI-driven transformations as well. AI-powered recommendation systems analyze customer behavior to suggest products that align with individual preferences, enhancing the shopping experience and driving sales. Inventory management systems use AI to predict demand and optimize stock levels, reducing waste and ensuring that products are available when customers need them. In customer service, AI chatbots provide immediate assistance, handling inquiries and resolving issues efficiently, which improves customer satisfaction and operational efficiency.

Transportation is another sector experiencing substantial changes due to AI. Autonomous vehicles, driven by AI technologies, promise to revolutionize logistics and personal transportation by increasing safety and reducing traffic congestion. AI systems manage traffic flows in real-time, optimizing signal timings and routing to alleviate congestion and improve travel times. Predictive maintenance powered by AI ensures that vehicles and infrastructure are serviced before issues become critical, reducing downtime and extending the lifespan of assets.

AI-enhanced decision-making represents a significant shift in how organizations approach strategic planning and operational efficiency. AI provides data-driven insights that support strategic decisions by analyzing vast amounts of data quickly and accurately. These insights enable leaders to make more informed decisions based on comprehensive information, identifying patterns, trends, and correlations that would be difficult for humans to discern. AI's ability to process and interpret data in real-time allows for timely and precise decision-making, which is crucial in fast-paced business environments.

AI supports strategic decisions by offering predictive analytics, which forecasts future outcomes based on historical data. This capability helps organizations anticipate market trends, customer behaviors, and potential challenges, allowing them to proactively adjust their strategies. For example, in marketing, AI can predict customer preferences and behaviors, enabling companies to tailor their campaigns more effectively and allocate resources efficiently. In operations, AI can optimize supply chain management by predicting demand fluctuations and optimizing inventory levels, reducing costs and improving service delivery.

Case studies of successful AI-driven decision-making processes illustrate the transformative potential of AI. In healthcare, AI systems such as IBM Watson Health have been used to support clinical decision-making. Watson analyzes medical records, scientific literature, and clinical guidelines to provide evidence-based treatment recommendations, helping doctors diagnose and treat diseases more accurately. This has led to improved patient outcomes and more efficient use of medical resources.

In finance, JPMorgan Chase implemented an AI system called COiN (Contract Intelligence) to analyze legal documents. COiN can review thousands of documents in seconds, identifying key terms and extracting relevant information. This significantly reduces the time and cost associated with manual document review and minimizes errors, leading to more efficient and accurate risk management.

Another example is the use of AI in retail by companies like Amazon. Amazon's AI-driven recommendation engine analyzes customer purchase history, browsing behavior, and preferences to suggest products that are most likely to interest each customer. This personalized approach not only enhances the customer experience but also drives sales and increases customer loyalty. The predictive analytics used in these recommendations help Amazon anticipate customer needs and optimize its inventory and supply chain accordingly.

The role of AI in risk management and predictive analytics is critical. AI systems can identify and assess risks by analyzing patterns and anomalies in data. In financial services, AI algorithms detect fraudulent transactions by monitoring real-time transaction data and flagging suspicious activities. This proactive approach helps prevent fraud and minimizes financial losses.

Predictive analytics powered by AI is also essential for managing operational risks. For example, in manufacturing, AI can predict equipment failures by analyzing sensor data and identifying patterns that precede breakdowns. This allows for predictive maintenance, where equipment is serviced before a failure occurs, reducing downtime and maintenance costs. In logistics, AI predicts delivery delays by analyzing weather patterns, traffic data, and other variables, enabling companies to adjust routes and schedules proactively.

AI presents numerous opportunities for innovation and growth across various sectors, fundamentally transforming how businesses develop products and services and engage with customers. One of the most significant opportunities lies in AI-driven product and service development. AI technologies enable companies to analyze vast amounts of data to identify market trends, consumer preferences, and emerging needs. This deep understanding allows for the creation of highly targeted and innovative products that resonate with specific customer segments. For instance, AI can analyze social media trends, customer reviews, and purchase histories to identify gaps in the market, inspiring the development of new products that meet these unaddressed demands.

AI also facilitates the rapid prototyping and testing of new products. Machine learning algorithms can simulate various scenarios and predict the performance of new products under different conditions, significantly reducing the time and cost associated with traditional product development cycles. This capability allows companies to experiment with more ideas and bring innovative products to market faster. For example, in the automotive industry, AI-driven simulations are used to design and test new vehicle models, optimizing performance, safety, and efficiency before physical prototypes are built.

AI is also driving innovation is through the enhancement of customer experiences. AI applications such as chatbots, virtual assistants, and personalized recommendation systems are transforming how businesses interact with their customers. These technologies provide instant, 24/7 customer support, handling inquiries, resolving issues, and offering personalized product recommendations. By analyzing customer data, AI systems can predict individual preferences and tailor interactions to meet specific needs, enhancing satisfaction and loyalty. Companies like Netflix and Spotify use AI algorithms to analyze viewing and listening habits, providing personalized content recommendations that keep users engaged and satisfied.

AI also enables businesses to offer more seamless and integrated customer experiences. For instance, in retail, AI-powered systems can track customer behavior both online and in-store, creating a unified profile that helps businesses understand and anticipate customer needs. This data-driven insight allows for the customization of marketing efforts, inventory management, and sales strategies to provide a more cohesive and satisfying shopping experience. Retail giants like Amazon use AI to optimize their supply chain, ensuring that products are available when and where customers want them, which enhances overall customer satisfaction.

AI opens up new opportunities for growth through its ability to optimize business operations and drive efficiency. AI-driven automation can handle repetitive and mundane tasks, freeing up human resources to focus on more strategic and creative activities. This not only improves operational efficiency but also fosters a more innovative work environment where employees can dedicate their time to problem-solving and ideation. For example, in financial services, AI automates tasks such as data entry, transaction processing, and compliance checks, allowing employees to focus on higher-value tasks like financial analysis and strategic planning.

AI's predictive analytics capabilities provide businesses with valuable insights that inform strategic decision-making. By analyzing historical data and identifying patterns, AI can forecast future trends and outcomes, enabling companies to make proactive decisions. This predictive power is particularly valuable in sectors such as healthcare, where AI can predict patient outcomes and optimize treatment plans, leading to better health results and operational efficiencies.

Ethical considerations and potential biases in AI systems are significant concerns. AI systems are only as good as the data they are trained on, and if this data contains biases, the AI can perpetuate and even amplify these biases. This can lead to unfair and discriminatory outcomes, particularly in sensitive areas such as hiring, lending, and law enforcement. For example, an AI system used for recruiting might favor candidates from certain demographics if the training data reflects historical biases in hiring practices. Addressing these biases requires careful selection and preprocessing of training data, as well as ongoing monitoring and testing of AI systems to ensure fairness and equity. Additionally, there must be transparency in how AI systems make decisions, allowing for accountability and the possibility to challenge and rectify biased outcomes.

Data privacy and security concerns are paramount in the age of AI. AI systems often rely on vast amounts of personal data to function effectively, raising significant privacy issues. Ensuring that this data is collected, stored, and processed in compliance with privacy laws such as GDPR and CCPA is essential. Moreover, data breaches and cyberattacks pose substantial risks, as they can compromise sensitive information and erode public trust. Robust data security measures, including encryption, secure access controls, and regular security audits, are necessary to protect against these threats. Furthermore, organizations must be transparent with users about how their data is used and provide them with control over their personal information.

Managing the transition to AI and addressing employee resistance is another critical challenge. The implementation of AI can lead to significant changes in job roles and workflows, causing anxiety and resistance among employees. Concerns about job displacement and the need for new skills can create fear and uncertainty. To manage this transition effectively, organizations must invest in reskilling and upskilling programs to prepare employees for new roles that leverage AI technologies. Communication is key; leaders must clearly articulate the benefits of AI, how it will enhance rather than replace human roles, and the support available for employees during the transition.

Fostering a culture of continuous learning and adaptability is crucial. Encouraging employees to embrace new technologies and providing opportunities for them to experiment and innovate with AI can help mitigate resistance. Involving employees in the AI adoption process, seeking their input, and addressing their concerns can also build buy-in and reduce resistance.

The changing nature of work and the workforce due to AI integration is a multifaceted phenomenon that significantly impacts job roles and employment patterns. AI technologies are automating routine and repetitive tasks across various industries, leading to shifts in the nature of many jobs. While AI can enhance productivity and efficiency, it also displaces certain roles, particularly those involving predictable and manual tasks. For instance, AI-powered chatbots and virtual assistants are handling customer service inquiries, reducing the need for human operators in these roles. Similarly, automated systems in manufacturing are performing assembly line tasks, leading to a decrease in demand for manual labor.

AI is not only eliminating jobs but also creating new opportunities. The demand for jobs that involve complex problem-solving, creativity, and emotional intelligence is increasing. AI technologies require skilled professionals for development, implementation, and maintenance. Roles in data science, machine learning, and AI ethics are growing rapidly. Additionally, AI is augmenting existing jobs by providing tools that enhance human capabilities, such as AI-driven analytics for better decision-making and automation of administrative tasks to allow professionals to focus on more strategic activities.

Reskilling and upskilling the workforce for the AI era is crucial to address these changes. As AI transforms job roles, workers need to acquire new skills to remain relevant and competitive. Reskilling involves training employees to transition into entirely new roles, while upskilling enhances their current capabilities to work alongside AI technologies. For example, factory workers might need to learn how to operate and maintain advanced robotic systems, while customer service representatives might be trained in managing complex queries that require human empathy and judgment, beyond what AI can handle.

Educational institutions and corporate training programs play a vital role in this reskilling and upskilling effort. Partnerships between businesses and educational providers can help develop tailored programs that meet the specific needs of the evolving job market. Online learning platforms and flexible learning modules enable workers to acquire new skills at their own pace, making education more accessible. Additionally, companies can invest in continuous learning initiatives, offering in-house training and development programs that keep their workforce up to date with the latest AI advancements.

Strategies for fostering a culture of continuous learning and adaptation are essential for organizations to thrive in the AI era. Leaders must champion the importance of lifelong learning and create an environment where employees feel encouraged and supported to pursue new skills. This can be achieved by embedding learning opportunities into the daily workflow, such as through microlearning sessions, on-the-job training, and access to online courses. Recognizing and rewarding employees who actively engage in learning and development can also motivate others to follow suit.

Fostering a growth mindset within the organization is critical. Encouraging employees to view challenges as opportunities for growth, and mistakes as learning experiences, helps build resilience and adaptability. Leaders should also facilitate open communication about the changes AI brings and involve employees in the AI adoption process. By seeking their input and addressing their concerns, leaders can build trust and reduce resistance to change.

Creating a collaborative learning environment where knowledge is shared freely among employees can further enhance the culture of continuous learning. Peer mentoring, cross-functional teams, and knowledge-sharing platforms can facilitate the exchange of ideas and expertise, fostering innovation and continuous improvement.

The future of AI-dominated life in business is poised to bring profound changes to leadership and organizational dynamics. Predictions and trends indicate that AI will continue to expand its influence across all aspects of business operations, fundamentally altering how leaders make decisions, strategize, and interact with their teams.

AI's future influence on leadership and business is expected to grow as technologies become more sophisticated and integrated into daily operations. AI will enable more precise and data-driven decision-making, allowing leaders to respond quickly to market changes and make informed strategic choices. Predictive analytics, enhanced by AI, will provide leaders with foresight into trends and potential disruptions, enabling proactive rather than reactive strategies. This shift will necessitate leaders who are not only comfortable with data and technology but also skilled in interpreting AI-generated insights to guide their organizations.

The evolving relationship between human leaders and AI technologies will likely become one of collaboration and augmentation. Rather than replacing human leaders, AI will serve as a powerful tool to enhance their capabilities. Leaders will increasingly rely on AI to handle routine tasks, analyze complex datasets, and generate actionable insights. This partnership will free leaders to focus on areas where human judgment and emotional intelligence are irreplaceable, such as building relationships, fostering innovation, and navigating ethical dilemmas. Successful leaders will be those who can effectively integrate AI into their leadership practices, leveraging its strengths while maintaining a human-centric approach.

Long-term implications for organizational structures and leadership roles will be significant. Traditional hierarchical models may give way to more fluid and adaptive structures that can respond rapidly to changes in the environment. AI can facilitate decentralized decision-making, empowering teams with the information and tools they need to make decisions autonomously. This could lead to flatter organizational structures where leadership is distributed, and decision-making is more collaborative.

Leadership roles will also evolve, with new positions emerging that focus on AI strategy and governance. Roles such as Chief AI Officer or AI Ethics Officer will become integral to ensuring that AI technologies are implemented responsibly and align with organizational values. These leaders will need to balance technical expertise with a deep understanding of ethical considerations, data privacy, and the societal impacts of AI. The integration of AI into business will drive a continuous need for learning and adaptation. Leaders will need to foster a culture that embraces change, encourages experimentation, and supports lifelong learning. This will involve providing ongoing education and development opportunities for employees to ensure they can effectively collaborate with AI technologies and stay ahead of the curve in an evolving job market.

As AI continues to permeate business processes, the distinction between technology and human work will blur. AI will be embedded into workflows, augmenting human capabilities and creating a seamless interaction between man and machine. This integration will enhance productivity, drive innovation, and enable organizations to tackle complex challenges more efficiently.

The future of AI-dominated life in business will be characterized by enhanced decision-making, collaborative human-AI relationships, and significant changes in organizational structures and leadership roles. Leaders who can effectively harness the power of AI while maintaining a focus on human-centric values will drive their organizations to new heights. As AI reshapes the business landscape, a commitment to continuous learning, ethical considerations, and adaptive strategies will be essential for navigating the opportunities and challenges that lie ahead.

Chapter 3: Ethical and Social Considerations

As AI technologies become increasingly integrated into business operations and daily life, a range of ethical concerns has emerged. Addressing these concerns is crucial for ensuring that AI development and deployment benefit society as a whole while minimizing potential harms. This section provides an overview of the key ethical issues associated with AI and the considerations that businesses and policymakers must address to navigate these challenges responsibly.

One of the most prominent ethical concerns with AI is bias and fairness. AI systems are trained on large datasets, and if these datasets contain biases, the AI models can perpetuate and even amplify these biases. This can lead to discriminatory outcomes in various applications, such as hiring, lending, and law enforcement. For example, an AI system used for recruitment might favor candidates from certain demographic groups over others if the training data reflects historical biases. Ensuring fairness in AI requires careful attention to the data used for training and the implementation of techniques to detect and mitigate biases. Transparency in AI decision-making processes is also essential, allowing stakeholders to understand how decisions are made and to hold systems accountable for their outcomes.

Data privacy is another critical ethical issue in the AI landscape. AI systems often require access to vast amounts of personal data to function effectively, raising concerns about how this data is collected, stored, and used. Individuals have a right to privacy, and businesses must navigate the tension between leveraging data for AI-driven insights and protecting personal information. Compliance with data protection regulations, such as the General Data Protection Regulation (GDPR) in Europe, is essential. Additionally, businesses should adopt best practices for data security and implement policies that ensure transparency and consent in data usage. Users should have control over their data, with clear options for opting in or out of data collection and usage.

The "black box" nature of many AI systems presents another ethical challenge. Complex AI models, particularly deep learning algorithms, often operate in ways that are not easily interpretable by humans. This lack of transparency can make it difficult to understand how AI systems arrive at their decisions, leading to challenges in accountability and trust. For instance, if an AI system denies a loan application, the applicant should be able to understand the reasons behind the decision. Enhancing the interpretability and explainability of AI models is an active area of research, aiming to develop methods that make AI decision-making processes more transparent and comprehensible to users.

The potential for job displacement due to AI-driven automation is a significant ethical and societal concern. As AI systems take over routine and repetitive tasks, there is a risk that certain job roles will become obsolete, leading to unemployment and economic disruption. Addressing this challenge requires proactive measures to support workers through the transition. Reskilling and upskilling programs are essential to help individuals acquire the skills needed for new roles created by AI technologies. Social safety nets and policies that promote inclusive growth and protect vulnerable populations are also crucial to mitigate the impact of job displacement.

Ethical concerns also extend to the potential misuse of AI technologies. AI can be used for malicious purposes, such as creating deepfakes, conducting cyber-attacks, or enabling surveillance and monitoring. The development and deployment of AI systems must include safeguards to prevent misuse and ensure that AI is used in ways that align with societal values and ethical principles. This includes implementing robust security measures, developing ethical guidelines for AI usage, and fostering a culture of ethical awareness among AI developers and users.

The environmental impact of AI is an emerging ethical issue that requires attention. Training large AI models consumes significant computational power, which in turn requires substantial energy resources. This energy consumption contributes to the carbon footprint of AI technologies, raising concerns about their sustainability. Businesses and researchers must explore ways to develop energy-efficient AI algorithms and leverage renewable energy sources to power AI computation. Additionally, optimizing the efficiency of AI models can reduce their environmental impact without compromising their performance.

Ensuring equitable access to AI technologies is another important ethical consideration. There is a risk that the benefits of AI could be concentrated among a few organizations or regions, exacerbating existing inequalities. Promoting inclusive innovation and ensuring that AI technologies are accessible to a broad range of stakeholders, including small businesses and developing countries, is essential for maximizing the societal benefits of AI. This involves supporting initiatives that democratize access to AI tools and resources and fostering collaborations that bridge gaps in AI capabilities.

The ethical use of AI also involves considering the broader societal implications of AI deployment. AI has the potential to reshape societal norms and values, influencing areas such as healthcare, education, and public policy. Engaging with diverse stakeholders, including ethicists, sociologists, and community representatives, can help ensure that AI technologies are developed and used in ways that align with societal goals and values. Public engagement and dialogue are crucial for building a consensus on the ethical principles that should guide AI development and deployment.

The ethical concerns associated with AI are multifaceted and require a comprehensive approach to address. Businesses, policymakers, and researchers must collaborate to develop ethical guidelines, implement robust governance frameworks, and foster a culture of ethical awareness in AI development and usage. By addressing issues such as bias, privacy, transparency, job displacement, misuse, environmental impact, equitable access, and societal implications, we can ensure that AI technologies are used responsibly and ethically, benefiting society as a whole. As we continue to explore the transformative potential of AI, it is essential to keep these ethical considerations at the forefront, guiding our efforts to create a future where AI contributes to the well-being and prosperity of all.

As AI systems become more integrated into various aspects of our lives, from hiring and lending to law enforcement and healthcare, concerns about bias and fairness in AI have come to the forefront. Understanding and addressing these issues is critical to ensuring that AI technologies promote equity and do not perpetuate or exacerbate existing inequalities.

AI bias originates primarily from the data used to train machine learning models. These models learn patterns and make predictions based on historical data. If the training data reflects existing biases in society, the AI system can learn and replicate these biases. For example, if an AI hiring tool is trained on historical data from a company that has predominantly hired male employees, the AI might learn to favor male candidates, perpetuating gender bias. Bias can also stem from the way data is collected and labeled. Incomplete or unrepresentative datasets can lead to biased outcomes. For instance, facial recognition systems trained predominantly on images of light-skinned individuals may perform poorly on individuals with darker skin tones, leading to disparities in accuracy and reliability.

There are several types of AI bias. Data bias occurs when the training data itself is biased, which can be due to historical inequalities, unbalanced datasets, or flawed data collection methods. Algorithmic bias arises when the algorithms used to process data introduce or amplify bias. Certain machine learning techniques might inherently favor patterns that align with existing biases. Measurement bias happens when the metrics used to evaluate AI performance are biased, skewing the system's outputs. Deployment bias occurs when an AI system trained on unbiased data exhibits bias when deployed in real-world scenarios where the operational environment differs from the training environment.

The consequences of AI bias are far-reaching and can have serious real-world implications. In hiring and employment, biased AI systems can result in unfair hiring practices, disadvantaging certain groups based on gender, race, or socioeconomic status. In criminal justice, AI systems used in law enforcement and criminal justice, such as predictive policing tools, can disproportionately target minority communities, perpetuating systemic biases. In healthcare, AI applications like diagnostic tools or personalized treatment plans can exhibit biases that lead to unequal treatment outcomes, affecting the quality of care received by different demographic groups. In financial services, biased AI systems in lending and credit scoring can result in discriminatory lending practices, denying loans or credit to qualified applicants based on biased criteria.

Mitigating AI bias involves several strategies. Ensuring that training datasets are diverse and representative of the populations the AI will serve is crucial. This includes actively seeking out underrepresented data and balancing datasets to prevent skewed outcomes. Implementing techniques to detect and mitigate bias during the development phase is essential, using fairness-aware algorithms, adjusting for known biases, and regularly auditing AI systems for bias. Enhancing the transparency and explainability of AI models helps stakeholders understand how decisions are made, building trust and accountability. Techniques like model interpretability, feature importance analysis, and providing clear explanations for AI decisions can help achieve this.

Inclusive design and development involve a diverse group of stakeholders in the AI development process, including those from marginalized communities. This can help identify and address potential biases early on. Adhering to regulatory and ethical standards for AI development and deployment is crucial, including complying with data protection regulations, implementing ethical AI guidelines, and participating in initiatives that promote fairness and accountability in AI. AI systems should be continuously monitored and evaluated for bias throughout their lifecycle, with models regularly updated with new data, fairness audits conducted, and systems adjusted based on feedback and performance assessments. Promoting awareness and education about AI bias among developers, data scientists, and decision-makers is vital, with training programs that highlight the ethical implications of AI and teach best practices for mitigating bias.

Government policies and regulations play a crucial role in addressing AI bias and ensuring fairness. Regulatory frameworks that mandate transparency, accountability, and non-discrimination in AI systems can provide a foundation for ethical AI practices. For example, the European Union's General Data Protection Regulation (GDPR) includes provisions that address algorithmic decision-making and bias, promoting greater transparency and accountability. Public sector initiatives, such as the establishment of AI ethics boards and the development of national AI strategies, can further support efforts to mitigate bias, providing guidelines for responsible AI development, promoting research into bias detection and mitigation techniques, and encouraging collaboration between industry, academia, and government.

Addressing AI bias is not just a technical challenge but an ethical imperative. Ensuring fairness in AI systems aligns with broader societal values of justice, equality, and human dignity. Ethical considerations should guide the entire AI development process, from data collection and model training to deployment and monitoring. Ethical AI practices involve recognizing and addressing the potential harms of biased AI systems, promoting inclusivity, and ensuring that AI technologies benefit all members of society. This includes prioritizing the well-being of marginalized and vulnerable populations, actively seeking to mitigate harm, and fostering an environment of ethical awareness and responsibility.

AI bias and fairness concerns are critical issues that must be addressed to ensure the responsible and equitable deployment of AI technologies. By understanding the origins and types of bias, implementing strategies to mitigate bias, and fostering a culture of ethical awareness, we can develop AI systems that promote fairness and inclusivity. Addressing these concerns is essential for building trust in AI technologies and ensuring that they contribute positively to society. As we continue to explore the transformative potential of AI, it is imperative to prioritize fairness and ethical considerations, guiding our efforts to create a future where AI benefits everyone.

AI systems rely on extensive datasets to function effectively, often including sensitive personal information such as financial records, health data, and personal communications. The collection, storage, and processing of this data raise critical privacy concerns. Individuals have a right to know how their data is being used, and they must have control over their personal information. Ensuring data privacy requires transparent data practices, including clear consent mechanisms and policies that explain what data is being collected and for what purpose.

Data security is another major concern. The large datasets used by AI systems are attractive targets for cyberattacks. Unauthorized access to this data can lead to significant harm, including identity theft, financial loss, and breaches of confidential information. Robust security measures are essential to protect AI datasets from hacking, breaches, and other cyber threats. This includes encryption, secure data storage, and regular security audits to identify and address vulnerabilities.

The use of AI in surveillance and monitoring also raises privacy issues. AI-powered surveillance systems can track individuals' movements, analyze their behavior, and recognize faces in public spaces. While these technologies can enhance security and safety, they also pose risks to privacy and civil liberties. The potential for misuse of surveillance data, such as unauthorized tracking or profiling of individuals, necessitates strict regulations and oversight to ensure that these systems are used ethically and responsibly.

Algorithmic transparency and accountability are crucial for addressing privacy and security concerns. Many AI systems operate as "black boxes," making decisions based on complex algorithms that are not easily understood by humans. This lack of transparency can lead to situations where individuals are unaware of how their data is being used or why certain decisions are made about them. Developing methods to enhance the interpretability of AI systems and providing clear explanations for AI-driven decisions can help build trust and accountability.

AI systems also pose challenges in terms of compliance with data protection regulations. Regulations such as the General Data Protection Regulation (GDPR) in Europe set stringent requirements for data privacy and security, including the right to access, correct, and delete personal data. AI systems must be designed and implemented in ways that comply with these regulations, ensuring that individuals' rights are protected. This includes implementing mechanisms for data anonymization, providing options for individuals to opt-out of data collection, and ensuring that data is processed lawfully and transparently.

The integration of AI into critical infrastructure, such as healthcare, finance, and transportation, further amplifies the importance of security. AI systems used in these sectors must be resilient to cyberattacks and other security threats. For example, AI-powered medical devices and diagnostic tools must be protected against tampering to ensure patient safety. Financial AI systems must guard against fraudulent activities and unauthorized access to sensitive financial data. Autonomous vehicles and transportation systems must be secure to prevent malicious interference that could endanger public safety.

Ethical considerations are also central to the privacy and security implications of AI. Ensuring that AI systems are designed and used in ways that respect individuals' privacy and security requires a commitment to ethical principles and responsible AI practices. This includes involving diverse stakeholders in the design and deployment of AI systems, conducting ethical impact assessments, and implementing governance frameworks that promote transparency, accountability, and fairness.

Organizations must also foster a culture of privacy and security awareness among their employees. Training programs that educate employees about data privacy, security best practices, and the ethical use of AI can help mitigate risks and promote responsible AI usage. Employees should be encouraged to adopt a proactive approach to privacy and security, recognizing potential threats and taking steps to protect sensitive information.

The potential for AI to be used in malicious ways, such as creating deepfakes or conducting cyberattacks, underscores the need for vigilance and proactive measures. Deepfakes, which use AI to create realistic but fake videos and images, can be used to spread misinformation, manipulate public opinion, and defame individuals. AI-powered cyberattacks can exploit vulnerabilities in systems, leading to data breaches and other security incidents. Addressing these risks requires ongoing research into AI security, the development of countermeasures, and collaboration between industry, government, and academia to stay ahead of emerging threats.

The privacy and security implications of AI are multifaceted and require a comprehensive approach to address. Protecting individuals' privacy, ensuring the security of AI systems, and fostering trust and accountability are essential for the responsible deployment of AI technologies. By implementing robust data protection measures, enhancing algorithmic transparency, complying with regulations, and promoting ethical AI practices, we can navigate the privacy and security challenges posed by AI and harness its potential for positive impact. As we continue to explore the transformative potential of AI, it is crucial to prioritize privacy and security, safeguarding the rights and well-being of individuals and organizations.

Artificial intelligence (AI) is not just a technological advancement but a transformative force that is reshaping societal values and norms. As AI systems become increasingly integrated into various aspects of life, they influence how we interact with technology, each other, and the world around us. Understanding the role of AI in shaping societal values and norms is crucial for ensuring that its development and deployment align with ethical principles and promote the well-being of society.

AI has the power to influence societal values by altering how we perceive and prioritize certain behaviors and practices. For instance, the widespread use of AI in surveillance and data collection can normalize the erosion of privacy. As people become accustomed to constant monitoring and data sharing, the societal expectation of privacy may diminish, leading to a shift in how privacy is valued and protected. This change in values can have profound implications for individual freedoms and civil liberties.

The integration of AI into decision-making processes also affects societal norms around accountability and transparency. AI systems, particularly those based on complex algorithms, often operate as "black boxes" with decisions that are not easily understandable by humans. This lack of transparency can erode trust in institutions that rely on AI, such as governments, healthcare providers, and financial institutions. To maintain trust, it is essential to develop AI systems that are transparent and provide clear explanations for their decisions, fostering a culture of accountability.

AI's influence extends to the workplace, where automation and AI-driven tools are changing the nature of work. The adoption of AI in various industries can lead to shifts in societal norms related to employment, productivity, and the value of human labor. As AI automates routine tasks, the demand for certain job roles may decrease, while new roles that require advanced technical skills and creativity emerge. This shift necessitates a reevaluation of educational priorities and workforce training programs to prepare individuals for the evolving job market. Societal norms around lifelong learning and continuous skill development will become increasingly important.

The deployment of AI in media and entertainment also shapes cultural values and norms. AI algorithms curate content on social media platforms, recommend movies and music, and even generate news articles. These AI-driven recommendations can create echo chambers, reinforcing existing beliefs and biases while limiting exposure to diverse perspectives. This phenomenon can influence public opinion and societal discourse, emphasizing the need for AI systems that promote balanced and diverse content.

In healthcare, AI is revolutionizing how medical decisions are made and treatments are personalized. AI-driven diagnostics, treatment planning, and predictive analytics can improve patient outcomes and make healthcare more efficient. However, the reliance on AI in healthcare also raises ethical questions about the doctor-patient relationship, informed consent, and the potential for algorithmic bias. Societal norms around trust in medical professionals and the acceptance of AI-driven healthcare solutions will continue to evolve.

AI's role in shaping societal values and norms is also evident in the legal and judicial systems. AI algorithms are increasingly used in predictive policing, risk assessment, and sentencing decisions. While these applications can improve efficiency and consistency, they also raise concerns about fairness, bias, and due process. The use of AI in the legal system challenges traditional norms of justice and accountability, necessitating robust safeguards and ethical guidelines to ensure that AI enhances rather than undermines the principles of justice.

The ethical use of AI is paramount in shaping societal values and norms. Developers, policymakers, and organizations must collaborate to establish ethical frameworks that guide AI development and deployment. These frameworks should prioritize fairness, transparency, accountability, and respect for human rights. Public engagement and dialogue are essential to ensure that diverse perspectives are considered and that AI systems reflect the values and needs of society.

Education plays a critical role in shaping how society interacts with AI. Increasing AI literacy among the general public can empower individuals to make informed decisions about their use of AI technologies and their implications. Educational programs that teach critical thinking, ethical reasoning, and technical skills related to AI can help individuals navigate the complexities of an AI-driven world and contribute to the responsible development and use of AI.

AI also has the potential to promote positive societal values by addressing global challenges. For example, AI can be used to combat climate change by optimizing energy use, reducing emissions, and predicting environmental impacts. AI-driven solutions can enhance public health by identifying disease outbreaks, improving healthcare delivery, and advancing medical research. By leveraging AI to address these and other societal challenges, we can promote values of sustainability, health, and well-being. AI plays a significant role in shaping societal values and norms. Its influence extends across various domains, from privacy and transparency to employment, media, healthcare, and justice. To ensure that AI's impact is positive and aligns with ethical principles, it is crucial to develop transparent, accountable, and fair AI systems. Public engagement, education, and ethical frameworks are essential for guiding the responsible use of AI and fostering societal values that promote the well-being of all individuals. As we navigate the complexities of AI integration, it is imperative to prioritize ethical considerations and work collaboratively to create a future where AI contributes to a just and equitable society.

Part II: Leadership in the AI Era

The advent of artificial intelligence is not only transforming industries but also fundamentally reshaping the nature of leadership. In this era of rapid technological advancement, leaders must evolve to meet new challenges and leverage AI's potential to drive innovation and efficiency. Traditional leadership models, which often emphasized hierarchical decision-making and rigid structures, are increasingly inadequate in a world where agility and adaptability are paramount.

Chapter 4 explores the need to redefine leadership in the AI age. Traditional approaches are limited in their ability to cope with the dynamic and fast-paced changes driven by AI. To lead effectively, there is a pressing need for leaders who are adaptive, agile, and innovative. Cultivating a growth mindset and embracing continuous learning are essential traits for leaders who aim to stay ahead of the curve and foster a culture of resilience and adaptability within their organizations.

Chapter 5 delves into the practical aspects of leading with AI. Integrating AI into leadership strategies and decision-making processes is crucial for harnessing its full potential. By leveraging AI for data-driven insights, leaders can make more informed decisions and optimize performance. This chapter also addresses the balance between human and AI capabilities, emphasizing the importance of combining the strengths of both to achieve optimal outcomes.

Chapter 6 focuses on building AI-powered organizations. Creating an AI-ready culture and mindset is fundamental for successful AI integration. This involves attracting, developing, and retaining AI talent and implementing effective governance and risk management frameworks to oversee AI deployment. By fostering an environment that supports innovation and ethical AI use, organizations can navigate the complexities of AI adoption and drive sustainable success.

As we explore these themes, this part of the book aims to provide leaders with the insights and tools needed to navigate the AI era with confidence and vision. By understanding and adapting to the transformative impact of AI, leaders can guide their organizations through this period of change and ensure they remain competitive and forward-thinking.

Chapter 4: Redefining Leadership

As artificial intelligence reshapes the landscape of business and society, traditional leadership models are increasingly being challenged. These models, often characterized by hierarchical decision-making, centralized authority, and linear thinking, are proving inadequate in an era defined by rapid technological advancements and constant change. The limitations of traditional leadership become evident when contrasted with the dynamic and fluid nature of the AI-driven world.

Traditional leadership models typically emphasize a top-down approach where decisions are made by a few individuals at the upper echelons of the organizational hierarchy. This model can lead to slow decision-making processes, as decisions must pass through multiple layers of approval. In contrast, the AI age demands swift and agile responses to rapidly changing market conditions and technological innovations. Hierarchical structures can impede the speed and flexibility needed to capitalize on AI-driven opportunities and address emerging challenges.

Centralized authority, another hallmark of traditional leadership, often limits the flow of information and stifles innovation. In a centralized system, critical decisions are made by a small group of leaders who may not have access to the most up-to-date or relevant information. This can result in decisions that are not fully informed by the latest data and insights. AI, with its ability to analyze vast amounts of data and provide real-time insights, requires a more decentralized approach where decision-making is distributed across the organization. Empowering employees at all levels to make data-driven decisions can lead to more innovative and effective outcomes.

Linear thinking, which focuses on predictable and incremental progress, is another limitation of traditional leadership models. AI and other emerging technologies often drive exponential change, creating environments where linear strategies are insufficient. Leaders who rely on past experiences and incremental improvements may struggle to keep pace with the disruptive nature of AI. The AI age requires leaders to think expansively and embrace uncertainty, exploring new possibilities and fostering a culture of experimentation and innovation.

Traditional leadership models often prioritize stability and control over adaptability and resilience. In a rapidly changing world, the ability to adapt to new circumstances and recover from setbacks is crucial. Traditional leaders may resist change and hold on to established practices, even when they are no longer effective. In contrast, adaptive leadership embraces change and seeks to learn from failures, viewing them as opportunities for growth and improvement.

The focus on individual leadership in traditional models can also be limiting. These models often emphasize the qualities and actions of a single leader, rather than the collective efforts of a team. In the AI age, collaborative leadership is essential. AI-driven projects typically require diverse teams with a range of skills and perspectives. Effective leaders must be able to foster collaboration, build cohesive teams, and leverage the collective intelligence of their organization. Traditional leadership models may lack the focus on ethical considerations that are crucial in the AI era. The deployment of AI raises significant ethical issues, including bias, privacy, and the impact on employment. Leaders must navigate these complexities with a strong ethical compass, ensuring that AI technologies are used responsibly and for the benefit of all stakeholders. This requires a commitment to transparency, accountability, and inclusivity, which may not be emphasized in traditional leadership approaches.

While these traditional leadership models have served organizations well in the past, their limitations are increasingly apparent in the AI age. The hierarchical, centralized, and linear approaches of traditional leadership are ill-suited to the dynamic, data-driven, and rapidly changing environment created by AI. To thrive in this new era, leaders must adopt more adaptive, decentralized, and collaborative approaches. By embracing these new models of leadership, organizations can better navigate the challenges and opportunities presented by AI, fostering innovation and ensuring sustainable success.

While these older leadership models face significant limitations in the AI age, new leadership paradigms are emerging to meet the demands of a rapidly evolving technological landscape. These models prioritize adaptability, collaboration, innovation, and ethical considerations, aligning with the dynamic nature of AI-driven environments. Here, we explore several contemporary leadership models that are particularly well-suited for leading organizations through the complexities and opportunities of the AI era.

Adaptive Leadership

Adaptive leadership is a model that emphasizes flexibility and responsiveness to change. Unlike traditional models that rely on rigid structures and processes, adaptive leadership encourages leaders to be open to new information and to adjust their strategies accordingly. This approach is particularly valuable in the AI age, where technological advancements and market conditions can shift rapidly. Adaptive leaders foster a culture of continuous learning and innovation, empowering their teams to experiment, take risks, and learn from failures. They prioritize resilience and the ability to pivot quickly in response to emerging trends and challenges.

Transformational Leadership

Transformational leadership focuses on inspiring and motivating employees to achieve their full potential and to embrace organizational goals. Transformational leaders create a vision for the future that leverages AI's potential to drive innovation and efficiency. They engage and empower their teams by fostering a sense of purpose and commitment. This model emphasizes the importance of building strong relationships, encouraging collaboration, and providing opportunities for professional growth. Transformational leaders are adept at navigating the complexities of AI by aligning their teams around a shared vision and fostering an environment that encourages creativity and innovation.

Servant Leadership

Servant leadership is a people-centric model that prioritizes the needs and development of employees. In the context of AI, servant leaders focus on supporting their teams through the transitions brought about by technological advancements. They invest in reskilling and upskilling programs to ensure that employees are equipped with the necessary skills to thrive in an AI-driven workplace. Servant leaders also emphasize ethical considerations, ensuring that AI is deployed in ways that benefit all stakeholders and uphold organizational values. By putting people first, servant leaders build trust, foster loyalty, and create a positive organizational culture that can navigate the challenges of AI integration.

Distributed Leadership

Distributed leadership, also known as shared or collaborative leadership, involves decentralizing decision-making and distributing leadership responsibilities across the organization. This model recognizes that in an AI-driven environment, valuable insights and expertise can come from all levels of the organization. Distributed leadership encourages collaboration and empowers employees to take initiative and make data-driven decisions. By leveraging the collective intelligence of the organization, distributed leadership fosters innovation and ensures that AI-driven insights are effectively integrated into business processes. This approach also enhances agility, enabling the organization to respond quickly to changes and capitalize on new opportunities.

Ethical Leadership

Ethical leadership is increasingly important in the AI age, where the deployment of AI technologies raises significant ethical issues. Ethical leaders prioritize transparency, accountability, and fairness in their decision-making processes. They are committed to ensuring that AI systems are designed and used in ways that are socially responsible and that respect the rights and dignity of all individuals. Ethical leaders engage with diverse stakeholders to understand the broader implications of AI and to develop guidelines and policies that promote ethical AI practices. By fostering a culture of integrity and ethical awareness, these leaders help build trust and credibility, both within the organization and with external stakeholders.

Agile Leadership

Agile leadership borrows principles from agile project management, emphasizing iterative development, customer collaboration, and flexibility. In an AI-driven world, agile leaders adopt a mindset that values adaptability and responsiveness. They encourage cross-functional teams to work collaboratively on AI projects, using iterative processes to test and refine AI applications. Agile leaders prioritize customer feedback and continuously seek to improve AI-driven products and services. This model supports rapid innovation and allows organizations to quickly adapt to evolving customer needs and technological advancements.

As AI continues to transform the business landscape, new leadership models are essential for navigating this complex and dynamic environment. Adaptive, transformational, servant, distributed, ethical, and agile leadership models offer valuable frameworks for leading organizations through the AI era. By embracing these contemporary approaches, leaders can foster innovation, build resilient and collaborative teams, and ensure that AI technologies are used responsibly and ethically. These new leadership paradigms will be crucial for organizations seeking to thrive in an AI-driven world, enabling them to harness the full potential of AI while navigating its challenges and opportunities.

The rapid advancement of AI technologies demands a new approach to leadership—one that is adaptive, agile, and innovative. In an era characterized by constant change and technological disruption, traditional leadership models fall short. Leaders must now navigate an environment where the pace of innovation is accelerating, and the ability to respond quickly to new challenges and opportunities is critical.

Adaptive leadership is essential in the AI age because it emphasizes flexibility and the capacity to evolve with changing circumstances. Adaptive leaders are not tied to a fixed set of strategies or practices; instead, they are open to new information and willing to adjust their approaches as needed. This mindset is crucial for integrating AI technologies, which often require iterative development and continuous learning to achieve their full potential.

Innovative leadership focuses on fostering creativity and encouraging the exploration of new ideas. AI presents numerous opportunities for innovation, from developing new products and services to transforming existing business models. Innovative leaders create environments where experimentation is encouraged, and failure is seen as a learning opportunity. They support their teams in thinking outside the box and pursuing novel solutions to complex problems.

Agile leadership, derived from agile project management principles, is particularly well-suited for the AI era. Agile leadership emphasizes iterative development, collaboration, flexibility, and responsiveness. Here, we delve deeper into the key practices and principles of agile leadership and how they can be effectively applied in the context of AI.

Agile leadership promotes the idea of iterative development, where projects are broken down into smaller, manageable increments. Each increment involves planning, execution, testing, and review, allowing teams to make continuous improvements based on feedback and results. This approach is highly effective for AI projects, which often involve complex algorithms and models that require refinement over time. By iterating on AI solutions, leaders can ensure that their teams are consistently enhancing performance and addressing any issues that arise.

One of the core tenets of agile leadership is the ability to be flexible and responsive to change. In the AI era, this means being able to pivot quickly when new data or insights become available or when market conditions shift. Agile leaders prioritize adaptability, encouraging their teams to embrace change rather than resist it. This flexibility is crucial for leveraging AI technologies, which can rapidly evolve and require organizations to stay nimble to maintain a competitive edge.

Agile leadership places a strong emphasis on collaboration and teamwork. AI projects often require the expertise of diverse professionals, including data scientists, engineers, domain experts, and business strategists. Agile leaders foster a collaborative environment where cross-functional teams can work together effectively. This collaboration enhances problem-solving capabilities and ensures that AI solutions are well-rounded and robust.

A strong focus on delivering value to customers is central to agile leadership. In the context of AI, this means developing solutions that meet customer needs and exceed their expectations. Agile leaders prioritize customer feedback and incorporate it into the development process, ensuring that AI products and services are aligned with user requirements. This customer-centric approach helps build trust and loyalty, as customers see that their needs are being addressed through innovative AI solutions.

Agile leaders empower their teams by granting them the autonomy to make decisions and take ownership of their work. This empowerment is critical for fostering innovation and agility. In AI projects, team members need the freedom to experiment with new ideas and approaches. Agile leaders provide the necessary support and resources while trusting their teams to drive the development process. This autonomy leads to higher engagement and motivation, as team members feel valued and empowered to contribute their best efforts.

Effective communication is a cornerstone of agile leadership. Agile leaders prioritize transparency, ensuring that all team members are informed about project goals, progress, and any changes that occur. Regular meetings, such as daily stand-ups and sprint reviews, facilitate open communication and help identify and address issues promptly. In AI projects, where collaboration and coordination are essential, transparent communication ensures that everyone is aligned and working towards common objectives.

Agile leadership encourages a proactive approach to risk management. In the AI era, where uncertainty and complexity are inherent, agile leaders identify potential risks early and develop strategies to mitigate them. This includes fostering a culture of experimentation, where taking calculated risks is encouraged. By testing new ideas and approaches in a controlled manner, agile teams can learn quickly and iterate on their solutions, reducing the likelihood of costly failures.

A commitment to continuous learning and development is emphasized in agile leadership. In the rapidly evolving field of AI, staying updated with the latest advancements and trends is crucial. Agile leaders support their teams in pursuing ongoing education and professional development opportunities. This commitment to learning ensures that team members have the skills and knowledge needed to innovate and excel in their roles.

Agile leadership practices are particularly well-suited for the AI era, where adaptability, collaboration, and continuous improvement are essential. By embracing iterative development, fostering a collaborative environment, and prioritizing customer-centric solutions, agile leaders can effectively navigate the complexities of AI integration. Empowerment, transparency, and a commitment to learning further enhance the ability of agile teams to innovate and respond to changing conditions. As organizations continue to leverage AI technologies, agile leadership will play a crucial role in driving success and maintaining a competitive edge in a dynamic and rapidly evolving landscape.

In the age of AI, the demand for authentic and transformative leadership skills has never been greater. As organizations navigate the complexities and opportunities presented by AI, leaders must possess qualities that go beyond traditional management practices. Authentic and transformative leadership is essential for fostering trust, driving innovation, and guiding organizations through rapid and often disruptive changes.

Authentic leadership is characterized by genuineness, transparency, and ethical behavior. Authentic leaders are true to themselves and their values, which inspires trust and loyalty among employees. In the context of AI, authenticity is crucial for several reasons. Firstly, AI implementation often involves significant changes to workflows, job roles, and organizational culture. Leaders who are transparent about these changes and their potential impacts can build trust and reduce resistance among employees. Secondly, ethical considerations are paramount when deploying AI technologies. Authentic leaders prioritize ethical decision-making, ensuring that AI systems are used responsibly and in ways that align with the organization's values and societal expectations.

Transformative leadership, on the other hand, focuses on inspiring and motivating employees to achieve their full potential and to embrace change. Transformative leaders create a vision for the future that leverages AI's potential to drive innovation and efficiency. They engage and empower their teams by fostering a sense of purpose and commitment. This model is particularly effective in the AI era, where continuous learning and adaptation are essential. Transformative leaders encourage experimentation and innovation, creating an environment where new ideas can flourish and employees feel empowered to take risks and explore novel solutions.

To lead effectively in the AI era, leaders must develop a range of skills that complement authentic and transformative leadership.

These skills are crucial for navigating the complexities of AI integration and driving organizational success in a rapidly evolving landscape.

Emotional Intelligence

Emotional intelligence (EQ) is the ability to understand and manage one's own emotions, as well as the emotions of others. In the AI age, EQ is vital for fostering strong interpersonal relationships and creating a positive organizational culture. Leaders with high EQ can navigate the emotional complexities of change management, support their teams through transitions, and build a collaborative and inclusive work environment. Emotional intelligence also enhances communication and conflict resolution, which are critical for effective teamwork and innovation.

Technological Literacy

While leaders do not need to be AI experts, a solid understanding of AI technologies and their potential applications is essential. Technological literacy enables leaders to make informed decisions about AI implementation, assess the feasibility of AI projects, and understand the implications of AI-driven insights. This knowledge also allows leaders to communicate effectively with technical teams and stakeholders, bridging the gap between technical and non-technical perspectives.

Strategic Thinking

Strategic thinking involves the ability to anticipate future trends, identify opportunities, and develop long-term plans that align with organizational goals. In the AI era, strategic thinking is crucial for leveraging AI to gain a competitive advantage. Leaders must be able to envision how AI can transform their industry, develop strategies for AI integration, and prioritize AI initiatives that drive value. Strategic thinking also involves risk management, ensuring that potential challenges and ethical considerations are addressed proactively.

Agility and Adaptability

The rapid pace of technological change requires leaders to be agile and adaptable. Agility involves the ability to pivot quickly in response to new information or changing circumstances. Adaptable leaders embrace uncertainty and are open to new ideas and approaches. In the context of AI, agility and adaptability enable leaders to respond effectively to technological advancements, market shifts, and evolving customer needs. This flexibility is essential for maintaining a competitive edge and driving continuous improvement.

Collaboration and Team Building

AI projects often require cross-functional collaboration, bringing together diverse teams with different expertise. Effective leaders must be skilled in building and leading collaborative teams, fostering a culture of teamwork, and leveraging the strengths of individual team members. Collaboration skills also involve facilitating open communication, encouraging knowledge sharing, and creating an environment where diverse perspectives are valued and integrated into decision-making processes.

Ethical and Inclusive Leadership

Ethical leadership is paramount in the AI era, where the deployment of AI technologies raises significant ethical issues. Leaders must prioritize fairness, transparency, accountability, and respect for human rights. This involves developing and implementing ethical guidelines for AI use, ensuring that AI systems are designed and deployed responsibly, and engaging with stakeholders to understand and address ethical concerns. Inclusive leadership goes hand-in-hand with ethical leadership, promoting diversity and inclusion within the organization. Inclusive leaders ensure that AI technologies are accessible to all employees and that diverse voices are represented in AI-related decisions.

The age of AI demands authentic and transformative leadership skills, combined with a range of competencies that enable leaders to navigate complexity and drive innovation. Emotional intelligence, technological literacy, strategic thinking, agility, collaboration, ethical and inclusive leadership, and a commitment to continuous learning are all critical for effective leadership in the AI era. By developing these skills, leaders can inspire their teams, foster a culture of innovation, and ensure that AI technologies are deployed responsibly and for the benefit of all stakeholders. These leadership qualities will be crucial for guiding organizations through the transformative impact of AI and achieving sustainable success in a rapidly changing world.

Cultivating a growth mindset and embracing continuous learning are essential for leaders and organizations striving to thrive amidst constant change and innovation. A growth mindset, a concept popularized by psychologist Carol Dweck, refers to the belief that abilities and intelligence can be developed through dedication, hard work, and the willingness to learn. This mindset contrasts with a fixed mindset, where individuals believe their abilities are static and unchangeable. In the context of AI, a growth mindset fosters an environment where experimentation, risk-taking, and learning from failure are encouraged.

Leaders with a growth mindset view challenges as opportunities for growth rather than threats. They understand that integrating AI technologies involves a steep learning curve and potential setbacks. Instead of being discouraged by these challenges, they see them as valuable experiences that contribute to personal and organizational development. This perspective is crucial for navigating the uncertainties and complexities of AI, where continuous adaptation and learning are necessary for success.

Embracing continuous learning is another key component of effective leadership in the AI age. The rapid pace of technological advancement means that knowledge and skills can quickly become outdated. Leaders must commit to lifelong learning, staying abreast of the latest developments in AI and related fields. This commitment involves seeking out new knowledge, acquiring new skills, and staying open to diverse perspectives. It also means encouraging and facilitating continuous learning within their teams, ensuring that employees have access to the resources and opportunities they need to develop their skills and stay competitive.

Creating a culture of continuous learning requires intentional effort from leaders. They must prioritize professional development, providing training programs, workshops, and access to educational resources. Encouraging employees to pursue further education, attend conferences, and participate in industry forums helps keep the organization at the forefront of AI advancements. Leaders should also foster a supportive environment where curiosity is valued and employees feel empowered to explore new ideas and technologies.

Mentorship and knowledge sharing are vital components of a learning culture. Leaders can act as mentors, guiding their teams and sharing their expertise and experiences. Encouraging peer-to-peer learning and collaboration helps disseminate knowledge throughout the organization and builds a cohesive, innovative workforce. Creating opportunities for employees to share their insights and successes promotes a culture of collective learning and continuous improvement.

Embracing a growth mindset and continuous learning also involves recognizing and celebrating progress, no matter how incremental. Leaders should acknowledge the efforts and achievements of their teams, reinforcing the value of persistence and dedication. This positive reinforcement encourages employees to remain engaged and motivated, even when faced with setbacks.

Leaders must model the behaviors they wish to see in their organizations. By demonstrating their own commitment to learning and growth, leaders set a powerful example for their teams. This includes being transparent about their learning journeys, openly discussing challenges and failures, and showing how they apply new knowledge to improve their performance and decision-making.

The ability to learn and adapt quickly is a significant competitive advantage. Organizations that cultivate a growth mindset and embrace continuous learning are better equipped to innovate, respond to market changes, and capitalize on new opportunities. This proactive approach to learning fosters resilience and agility, enabling organizations to thrive in an environment characterized by rapid technological evolution. The AI age necessitates authentic and transformative leadership skills, with a strong emphasis on a growth mindset and continuous learning. By fostering an environment where challenges are seen as opportunities, and continuous improvement is prioritized, leaders can drive innovation and ensure their organizations remain competitive. Emotional intelligence, technological literacy, strategic thinking, agility, collaboration, ethical and inclusive leadership, and a commitment to lifelong learning are all critical for effective leadership in this new era. By developing these skills and cultivating a culture of growth and learning, leaders can guide their organizations through the transformative impact of AI, achieving sustainable success and positioning themselves for the future.

Chapter 5: Leading with AI

In the age of artificial intelligence, integrating AI into leadership strategies and decision-making processes is crucial for organizations aiming to maintain a competitive edge and drive innovation. AI has the potential to transform how leaders gather insights, make decisions, and implement strategies. Effective integration of AI can enhance efficiency, accuracy, and strategic vision, enabling leaders to navigate the complexities of the modern business landscape.

The first step in integrating AI into leadership strategies is understanding the capabilities and limitations of AI technologies. Leaders must be well-versed in the basics of AI, including machine learning, data analytics, and natural language processing, to make informed decisions about how to leverage these tools. This foundational knowledge allows leaders to identify the most suitable AI applications for their organization and understand how AI can complement and enhance human decision-making.

One of the primary benefits of AI is its ability to process vast amounts of data quickly and accurately. By leveraging AI for data analysis, leaders can gain deeper insights into market trends, customer behavior, and operational performance. This data-driven approach enables leaders to make more informed and evidence-based decisions, reducing reliance on intuition and guesswork. AI-driven analytics can uncover patterns and correlations that might be overlooked by human analysis, providing a more comprehensive understanding of the business environment.

AI can also enhance strategic planning by providing predictive insights. Predictive analytics, powered by AI, can forecast future trends and outcomes based on historical data and current variables. This capability is invaluable for strategic decision-making, as it allows leaders to anticipate market shifts, identify emerging opportunities, and mitigate potential risks. By incorporating predictive insights into their strategic planning, leaders can make proactive decisions that position their organizations for long-term success.

Another significant advantage of AI is its ability to automate routine and repetitive tasks. This automation frees up leaders and their teams to focus on higher-value activities that require creativity, critical thinking, and strategic insight. For example, AI can handle data collection, preliminary analysis, and reporting, allowing leaders to concentrate on interpreting results and making strategic decisions. Automation also enhances efficiency and accuracy, reducing the likelihood of human error and ensuring that decisions are based on reliable data.

AI-powered decision support systems can assist leaders in complex decision-making processes. These systems use advanced algorithms to evaluate multiple scenarios, weigh potential outcomes, and recommend optimal courses of action. By integrating AI into decision support, leaders can explore various options and make well-informed choices that align with their strategic goals. AI can also provide real-time recommendations, enabling leaders to respond swiftly to changing conditions and emerging challenges.

Integrating AI into leadership strategies also involves fostering a culture that embraces AI and data-driven decision-making. Leaders must promote the adoption of AI tools and technologies across the organization, ensuring that employees at all levels understand the benefits and applications of AI. This cultural shift requires effective communication, training, and support to build confidence and competence in using AI-driven insights. Encouraging a collaborative approach, where AI and human intelligence complement each other, enhances the overall decision-making process and drives innovation.

Transparency and ethical considerations are critical when integrating AI into leadership strategies. Leaders must ensure that AI systems are transparent and explainable, providing clear insights into how decisions are made. This transparency builds trust and accountability, both within the organization and with external stakeholders. Additionally, ethical guidelines must be established to govern the use of AI, addressing issues such as bias, privacy, and fairness. By prioritizing ethical AI practices, leaders can mitigate risks and ensure that AI technologies are used responsibly and for the benefit of all stakeholders.

The integration of AI into leadership strategies and decision-making processes also requires a commitment to continuous learning and adaptation. As AI technologies evolve, leaders must stay informed about the latest advancements and best practices. This ongoing education enables leaders to leverage new AI capabilities and ensure that their strategies remain relevant and effective. Encouraging a culture of continuous improvement, where feedback and learning are integral to the decision-making process, helps organizations stay agile and responsive to change.

Integrating AI into leadership strategies and decision-making processes offers significant advantages, including enhanced data analysis, predictive insights, automation, and decision support. To achieve these benefits, leaders must understand AI technologies, promote a data-driven culture, ensure transparency and ethical practices, and commit to continuous learning. By effectively leveraging AI, leaders can make more informed and strategic decisions, drive innovation, and position their organizations for success in the rapidly evolving AI landscape.

AI continues to revolutionize various aspects of business and society, cultivating an AI-ready mindset is essential for leaders and organizations aiming to thrive in this transformative era. An AI-ready mindset encompasses a range of attitudes and behaviors that enable individuals and teams to effectively integrate and leverage AI technologies. Key components of this mindset include fostering a growth mindset and openness to change, encouraging curiosity, experimentation, and risk-taking, addressing fears and resistance to AI adoption, and promoting a culture of continuous learning and adaptation.

Fostering a growth mindset and openness to change is fundamental for an AI-ready mindset. A growth mindset, which emphasizes the belief that abilities and intelligence can be developed through dedication and hard work, is crucial for navigating the challenges and opportunities presented by AI. Leaders with a growth mindset view AI as an opportunity for growth and innovation rather than a threat. They are open to new ideas and willing to adapt their strategies in response to technological advancements. This openness to change is essential for successfully integrating AI into organizational processes and ensuring that teams remain agile and responsive to evolving demands.

Encouraging curiosity, experimentation, and risk-taking is another critical aspect of cultivating an AI-ready mindset. AI technologies offer numerous possibilities for innovation, but realizing their full potential requires a willingness to explore and experiment with new approaches. Leaders should foster an environment where curiosity is valued and employees feel empowered to ask questions, seek out new knowledge, and experiment with AI applications. This involves creating opportunities for hands-on learning and experimentation, where teams can test new ideas, learn from failures, and iterate on their solutions. By promoting a culture of curiosity and risk-taking, organizations can drive innovation and uncover new ways to leverage AI.

Addressing fears and resistance to AI adoption is essential for building an AI-ready mindset. Resistance to AI often stems from fears about job displacement, loss of control, and the unknown implications of new technologies. Leaders must acknowledge these concerns and provide clear, transparent communication about the role of AI within the organization. This involves explaining how AI will be used, the benefits it can bring, and the steps being taken to mitigate potential risks. Providing training and support to help employees develop new skills and adapt to AI-driven changes can also alleviate fears and build confidence in using AI technologies. By addressing resistance proactively and fostering a supportive environment, leaders can facilitate smoother AI adoption and integration.

Promoting a culture of continuous learning and adaptation is crucial for maintaining an AI-ready mindset. The rapid pace of AI advancements means that knowledge and skills must be continually updated to stay relevant. Leaders should encourage a commitment to lifelong learning, providing access to educational resources, training programs, and professional development opportunities. This commitment to continuous learning ensures that employees are equipped with the latest knowledge and skills needed to leverage AI effectively. It also fosters a culture of adaptability, where teams are prepared to embrace change and continuously improve their processes and solutions.

Creating opportunities for collaboration and knowledge sharing is also vital for an AI-ready mindset. AI projects often require diverse expertise and perspectives, making collaboration essential for success. Leaders should encourage cross-functional teamwork and create platforms for employees to share their insights, experiences, and best practices. This collaborative approach not only enhances the quality of AI solutions but also builds a sense of community and collective learning within the organization.

Cultivating an AI-ready mindset involves fostering a growth mindset and openness to change, encouraging curiosity, experimentation, and risk-taking, addressing fears and resistance to AI adoption, and promoting a culture of continuous learning and adaptation. By developing these attitudes and behaviors, leaders can effectively integrate AI technologies, drive innovation, and position their organizations for success in the AI era. An AI-ready mindset enables organizations to navigate the complexities and opportunities of AI, ensuring that they remain agile, resilient, and competitive in a rapidly evolving landscape. As AI becomes increasingly integrated into organizational operations, there is a pressing need to redesign leadership roles and responsibilities to fully leverage the benefits of human-AI collaboration. This involves redefining leadership roles, identifying tasks to delegate to AI systems, empowering leaders to focus on strategic and creative aspects, and promoting new leadership competencies suited for the AI era.

Redefining leadership roles in the context of human-AI collaboration is essential for maximizing the potential of AI technologies. Traditional leadership roles often involve a significant amount of time spent on routine decision-making, data analysis, and operational oversight. With AI systems capable of handling many of these tasks more efficiently, leaders can redefine their roles to focus more on areas where human judgment, creativity, and emotional intelligence are paramount. This shift allows leaders to concentrate on strategic vision, long-term planning, and fostering innovation within their teams. It also means that leaders need to become adept at managing and integrating AI systems into their workflows, ensuring that AI augments rather than replaces human capabilities.

Identifying tasks and responsibilities to delegate to AI systems is a crucial step in this process. AI excels at processing large volumes of data, identifying patterns, and making predictions based on historical trends. Routine tasks such as data entry, scheduling, and preliminary data analysis can be effectively handled by AI, freeing up leaders to focus on higher-value activities. Additionally, AI can assist in more complex decision-making processes by providing insights and recommendations based on sophisticated algorithms. By delegating these tasks to AI, leaders can reduce the cognitive load on themselves and their teams, allowing them to dedicate more time and energy to strategic thinking and creative problem-solving.

Empowering leaders to focus on strategic, creative, and human-centric aspects of their roles is essential for driving organizational success in the AI era. Strategic leadership involves setting a vision for the future, identifying opportunities for growth, and developing plans to achieve organizational goals. AI can support these efforts by providing data-driven insights and predictive analytics, but the ultimate responsibility for strategic direction lies with human leaders. Creativity and innovation are also critical components of leadership in the AI age. Leaders must foster a culture that encourages experimentation, embraces new ideas, and supports risk-taking. This involves creating an environment where team members feel safe to explore and innovate, knowing that their contributions are valued and supported.

Human-centric leadership focuses on the interpersonal and ethical dimensions of leadership. AI systems, while powerful, lack the ability to understand and respond to human emotions and social nuances. Leaders must excel in areas such as empathy, communication, and ethical decision-making. They need to build strong relationships with their teams, provide support and guidance, and ensure that AI is used responsibly and ethically. This human-centric approach is crucial for maintaining trust and morale within the organization, especially as AI technologies continue to evolve and impact the workplace.

Promoting new leadership competencies for the AI era is essential for preparing leaders to navigate the complexities of AI integration. Key competencies include technological literacy, strategic agility, emotional intelligence, and ethical leadership. Technological literacy involves understanding the capabilities and limitations of AI, as well as staying informed about the latest advancements in the field. Strategic agility refers to the ability to adapt quickly to changing conditions and to pivot strategies in response to new information and opportunities. Emotional intelligence encompasses the skills needed to understand and manage one's own emotions and the emotions of others, fostering strong interpersonal relationships and effective teamwork. Ethical leadership involves making decisions that are aligned with organizational values and societal norms, ensuring that AI is used in ways that are fair, transparent, and accountable.

In addition to these competencies, leaders must also develop skills in managing AI systems and data-driven decision-making. This includes understanding how to interpret AI-generated insights, integrating these insights into strategic planning, and monitoring the performance of AI systems to ensure they are delivering the desired outcomes. Leaders must also be adept at communicating the benefits and limitations of AI to their teams and stakeholders, building confidence and trust in the technology.

Redesigning leadership roles and responsibilities in the AI era involves redefining leadership in the context of human-AI collaboration, identifying tasks to delegate to AI, empowering leaders to focus on strategic and creative aspects, and promoting new competencies suited for the AI age. By embracing these changes, leaders can effectively leverage AI technologies to enhance organizational performance, drive innovation, and maintain a human-centric approach to leadership. This transformation is crucial for navigating the complexities of the AI-driven world and ensuring sustainable success in a rapidly evolving landscape.

The ability to leverage data-driven insights for informed decision-making is a critical leadership skill. AI technologies enable leaders to process vast amounts of data quickly and accurately, uncovering patterns and trends that inform strategic decisions. By integrating AI into decision-making processes, organizations can enhance their strategic vision, optimize operations, and drive innovation.

One of the primary benefits of AI is its capacity to analyze large datasets and generate actionable insights. Traditional methods of data analysis are often time-consuming and limited in scope. AI, particularly machine learning algorithms, can handle complex and voluminous data sets, identifying correlations and trends that might not be apparent through manual analysis. These insights can inform a wide range of decisions, from operational adjustments to long-term strategic planning. For example, AI can enhance market analysis by identifying emerging trends and shifts in consumer behavior. By analyzing social media activity, customer feedback, and sales data, AI systems can provide real-time insights into market dynamics. These insights enable leaders to anticipate changes, adjust marketing strategies, and tailor products or services to meet evolving customer needs. This proactive approach helps organizations stay competitive and responsive to market demands.

In operations, AI can optimize processes by identifying inefficiencies and recommending improvements. For instance,

AI-powered predictive maintenance systems can analyze data from machinery and equipment to predict when maintenance is needed, reducing downtime and extending the lifespan of assets. Similarly, AI can optimize supply chain management by analyzing logistics data to predict demand, manage inventory levels, and streamline distribution. These operational efficiencies translate into cost savings and enhanced productivity. AI also plays a crucial role in enhancing customer experiences. By analyzing customer data, AI can personalize interactions and tailor recommendations to individual preferences. AI-driven chatbots and virtual assistants can provide instant customer support, resolving issues and answering queries with high accuracy. This level of personalization and responsiveness builds customer loyalty and satisfaction, driving business growth.

For strategic decision-making, AI offers predictive analytics that forecast future trends based on historical data. These predictive models can inform a wide range of strategic decisions, from financial planning to resource allocation. For example, AI can forecast sales trends, helping leaders set realistic revenue targets and budget allocations. In human resources, AI can predict employee turnover, enabling proactive measures to improve retention and engagement. By leveraging predictive analytics, leaders can make data-driven decisions that align with long-term goals and mitigate potential risks.

Integrating AI into decision-making processes also involves using AI as a decision support tool. AI systems can evaluate multiple scenarios and recommend optimal courses of action based on data analysis. For example, in financial services, AI can assess investment options and suggest portfolios that balance risk and return. In healthcare, AI can analyze patient data to recommend treatment plans that optimize outcomes. By providing data-driven recommendations, AI enhances the quality and accuracy of decisions, reducing the reliance on intuition and guesswork. Leveraging AI for decision-making requires a commitment to data quality and integrity. AI systems are only as good as the data they analyze. Ensuring that data is accurate, complete, and representative is crucial for generating reliable insights. Leaders must invest in robust data governance practices, including data cleaning, validation, and management. This ensures that AI systems have access to high-quality data, enhancing their analytical capabilities and the reliability of their insights.

Transparency and explainability are also essential when using AI for decision-making. AI systems, particularly deep learning models, can sometimes operate as "black boxes," making it difficult to understand how they arrive at their conclusions. Leaders must prioritize transparency, ensuring that AI systems provide clear explanations for their recommendations. This builds trust in AI-driven insights and enables leaders to make informed decisions with confidence.

Ethical considerations must also be at the forefront of leveraging AI for decision-making. Ensuring that AI systems are free from bias and that their use complies with ethical standards and regulations is paramount. Leaders must establish ethical guidelines for AI use, addressing issues such as data privacy, fairness, and accountability. By promoting ethical AI practices, leaders can mitigate risks and ensure that AI technologies are used responsibly and for the benefit of all stakeholders.

Leveraging AI for data-driven insights and informed decision-making offers significant advantages for organizations. AI enables leaders to process large datasets, uncover actionable insights, and make decisions that enhance strategic vision, optimize operations, and drive innovation. To achieve these benefits, leaders must ensure data quality, prioritize transparency, and uphold ethical standards. By integrating AI into their decision-making processes, leaders can navigate the complexities of the AI era and position their organizations for sustained success in a rapidly evolving landscape.

Achieving optimal performance requires a harmonious balance between human and AI capabilities. While AI technologies offer powerful tools for data analysis, automation, and decision-making, human skills such as creativity, emotional intelligence, and ethical judgment remain irreplaceable. Integrating AI with human expertise allows organizations to leverage the strengths of both, creating a synergistic environment that drives innovation, efficiency, and sustainable success.

The first step in balancing human and AI capabilities is recognizing the distinct strengths each brings to the table. AI excels at processing large volumes of data rapidly, identifying patterns, and making predictions based on historical trends. These capabilities are invaluable for tasks that involve data analysis, routine decision-making, and operational efficiency. For example, AI can analyze customer data to identify purchasing trends, automate repetitive tasks such as scheduling and reporting, and provide predictive maintenance insights for machinery. On the other hand, humans possess unique abilities that AI cannot replicate. Creativity, critical thinking, empathy, and ethical reasoning are areas where human judgment is essential. Leaders and employees can interpret AI-generated insights within the broader context of organizational goals and values, make nuanced decisions that consider ethical implications, and innovate by thinking outside the box. Human creativity drives the development of new products, services, and business models that AI systems alone could not conceive.

To effectively balance human and AI capabilities, organizations must foster a culture of collaboration where both are seen as complementary rather than competing forces. This involves redefining roles and responsibilities to ensure that AI is used to augment human abilities, not replace them. For instance, while AI can handle data analysis, humans should interpret the results, make strategic decisions, and communicate these insights across the organization.

Empowering employees with the skills to work alongside AI is crucial. This includes providing training on how to use AI tools effectively, understanding AI's limitations, and developing the ability to critically assess AI-generated insights. Employees should be encouraged to develop digital literacy and data analysis skills, enabling them to leverage AI tools to enhance their work. Additionally, fostering a mindset that embraces AI as a collaborative partner can help reduce resistance and increase acceptance of AI technologies within the organization.

Leaders play a pivotal role in balancing human and AI capabilities. They must set a vision for how AI will be integrated into the organization, communicate this vision clearly, and ensure that it aligns with the company's values and goals. Leaders should also promote a culture of continuous learning and adaptation, encouraging employees to stay updated with AI advancements and explore new ways to incorporate AI into their workflows. By demonstrating a commitment to leveraging both human and AI capabilities, leaders can inspire their teams to embrace this balanced approach.

Effective collaboration between humans and AI also requires robust data governance and ethical frameworks. Ensuring that AI systems operate transparently and fairly is essential for building trust. Organizations must implement practices that prevent bias in AI algorithms, protect data privacy, and ensure accountability in AI-driven decisions. By upholding high ethical standards, organizations can mitigate risks and foster a positive relationship between human employees and AI technologies.

Another critical aspect of balancing human and AI capabilities is the iterative process of feedback and improvement. AI systems should be continuously monitored and refined based on user feedback and evolving organizational needs. Humans play a vital role in this process by providing insights into how AI tools are performing, identifying areas for improvement, and suggesting new applications for AI technologies. This feedback loop ensures that AI systems remain relevant and effective while adapting to the changing landscape of the organization.

Encouraging cross-functional teams that bring together diverse skill sets can also enhance the integration of human and AI capabilities. These teams can include data scientists, engineers, business strategists, and frontline employees who work together to develop and implement AI solutions. This collaborative approach ensures that AI tools are designed and deployed with a holistic understanding of the organization's objectives and challenges.

Balancing human and AI capabilities for optimal performance involves recognizing the unique strengths of each, fostering a culture of collaboration, empowering employees with the necessary skills, and promoting ethical and transparent AI practices. By integrating AI to augment human abilities rather than replace them, organizations can enhance efficiency, drive innovation, and achieve sustainable success. Leaders play a crucial role in setting the vision, promoting continuous learning, and ensuring that AI technologies are used responsibly. Through this balanced approach, organizations can navigate the complexities of the AI era and harness the full potential of both human and AI capabilities.

Chapter 6: Building AI-Powered Organizations

As AI continues to reshape industries and redefine business practices, fostering an AI-ready culture and mindset within an organization is essential. An AI-ready culture embraces change, values data-driven decision-making, encourages continuous learning, and fosters collaboration between humans and AI. Cultivating this mindset involves several key steps, including promoting a growth mindset, encouraging curiosity and experimentation, addressing fears and resistance to AI adoption, and fostering a culture of continuous learning and adaptation.

Promoting a growth mindset is foundational to developing an AI-ready culture. A growth mindset, as defined by psychologist Carol Dweck, is the belief that abilities and intelligence can be developed through effort, learning, and perseverance. In the context of AI, a growth mindset helps employees and leaders view AI as a tool for growth and innovation rather than a threat. Leaders can promote this mindset by encouraging employees to embrace challenges, learn from failures, and continuously seek opportunities for improvement. This approach fosters resilience and adaptability, both of which are crucial for successfully integrating AI technologies.

Encouraging curiosity and experimentation is another critical component of an AI-ready culture. AI technologies offer immense potential for innovation, but realizing this potential requires a willingness to explore new ideas and take risks. Leaders should create an environment where curiosity is valued, and employees feel empowered to ask questions, seek new knowledge, and experiment with AI applications. Providing opportunities for hands-on learning and experimentation, such as hackathons, innovation labs, and pilot projects, allows teams to test new ideas, learn from their experiences, and iterate on their solutions.

Addressing fears and resistance to AI adoption is essential for fostering a positive attitude towards AI within the organization. Resistance often stems from concerns about job displacement, loss of control, and the unknown implications of new technologies. Leaders must acknowledge these fears and provide clear, transparent communication about the role of AI within the organization. This involves explaining how AI will be used, the benefits it can bring, and the steps being taken to mitigate potential risks. Providing training and support to help employees develop new skills and adapt to AI-driven changes can also alleviate fears and build confidence in using AI technologies.

Fostering a culture of continuous learning and adaptation is crucial for maintaining an AI-ready mindset. The rapid pace of AI advancements means that knowledge and skills must be continually updated to stay relevant. Leaders should encourage a commitment to lifelong learning, providing access to educational resources, training programs, and professional development opportunities. This commitment ensures that employees are equipped with the latest knowledge and skills needed to leverage AI effectively. It also fosters a culture of adaptability, where teams are prepared to embrace change and continuously improve their processes and solutions.

Creating opportunities for collaboration and knowledge sharing is also vital for an AI-ready culture. AI projects often require diverse expertise and perspectives, making collaboration essential for success. Leaders should encourage cross-functional teamwork and create platforms for employees to share their insights, experiences, and best practices. This collaborative approach not only enhances the quality of AI solutions but also builds a sense of community and collective learning within the organization.

Leaders play a pivotal role in fostering an AI-ready culture by modeling the behaviors they wish to see in their teams. By demonstrating their own commitment to learning and growth, leaders set a powerful example for their employees. This includes being transparent about their learning journeys, openly discussing challenges and failures, and showing how they apply new knowledge to improve their performance and decision-making. Additionally, implementing robust data governance practices is essential for building trust in AI systems. Ensuring data quality, accuracy, and integrity is critical for generating reliable AI insights. Leaders must establish clear data governance frameworks, including data privacy policies, ethical guidelines, and mechanisms for monitoring and addressing bias in AI algorithms. By upholding high standards of data governance, organizations can build confidence in their AI systems and promote ethical and responsible AI use.

Recognizing and celebrating progress, no matter how incremental, is also important for fostering an AI-ready culture. Leaders should acknowledge the efforts and achievements of their teams, reinforcing the value of persistence and dedication. This positive reinforcement encourages employees to remain engaged and motivated, even when faced with setbacks.

Fostering an AI-ready culture and mindset involves promoting a growth mindset, encouraging curiosity and experimentation, addressing fears and resistance, and fostering a culture of continuous learning and adaptation. Leaders play a crucial role in setting the tone, providing support, and modeling the desired behaviors. By creating an environment that values learning, collaboration, and innovation, organizations can effectively integrate AI technologies and navigate the complexities of the AI era. This AI-ready culture ensures that employees are equipped to leverage AI's full potential, driving innovation, efficiency, and sustainable success.

Developing an AI-centric workforce is crucial for organizations aiming to stay competitive and innovative. An AI-centric workforce is not only skilled in leveraging AI technologies but also adaptable, collaborative, and committed to continuous learning. Building such a workforce involves attracting and developing AI talent, fostering an AI-ready culture, implementing effective AI governance and risk management frameworks, and ensuring continuous education and skill development.

To build an AI-centric workforce, organizations must first attract and recruit individuals with expertise in AI and related fields. This includes data scientists, machine learning engineers, AI researchers, and professionals with strong analytical and computational skills. Organizations should create compelling value propositions that highlight opportunities for innovation, career growth, and the chance to work on cutting-edge technologies. Competitive compensation packages, flexible work arrangements, and a positive workplace culture are also important factors in attracting top AI talent.

Once talented individuals are onboard, it's essential to invest in their development. Providing comprehensive onboarding programs that include training in the organization's AI tools, systems, and processes can help new hires hit the ground running. Mentorship programs and career development plans that outline clear paths for advancement can also motivate employees and help retain top talent. Encouraging employees to pursue certifications, attend conferences, and participate in professional networks can further enhance their skills and knowledge.

An AI-centric workforce thrives in an environment that values innovation, collaboration, and continuous learning. Fostering an AI-ready culture involves promoting a growth mindset, where employees are encouraged to embrace challenges, learn from failures, and continuously seek improvement. Leaders should model these behaviors, demonstrating their own commitment to learning and growth.

Encouraging curiosity and experimentation is crucial for driving innovation. Organizations should create opportunities for employees to experiment with AI technologies, such as hackathons, innovation labs, and pilot projects. Providing a safe space for risk-taking and learning from mistakes can foster a culture of creativity and exploration.

Effective AI governance and risk management frameworks are essential for ensuring that AI technologies are used responsibly and ethically. This involves establishing clear guidelines and policies for AI development and deployment, including data privacy, security, and ethical considerations. Organizations should implement processes for monitoring and addressing biases in AI algorithms, ensuring that AI systems operate fairly and transparently.

Leaders must also ensure compliance with relevant regulations and standards, such as the General Data Protection Regulation (GDPR) and other data protection laws. Regular audits and assessments of AI systems can help identify potential risks and areas for improvement. By prioritizing ethical AI practices, organizations can build trust with their employees, customers, and other stakeholders.

The rapid pace of AI advancements requires a commitment to continuous education and skill development. Organizations should provide access to educational resources, training programs, and professional development opportunities to help employees stay updated with the latest AI technologies and trends. This includes offering courses in machine learning, data science, and AI ethics, as well as hands-on training with AI tools and platforms.

Encouraging employees to pursue advanced degrees, certifications, and industry credentials can further enhance their expertise. Partnerships with academic institutions, research organizations, and industry groups can provide additional learning opportunities and access to cutting-edge research. Creating a learning environment that supports peer-to-peer knowledge sharing and collaboration is also important. Regular workshops, seminars, and knowledge-sharing sessions can facilitate the exchange of ideas and best practices. Leaders should encourage employees to share their insights and experiences, fostering a culture of collective learning and continuous improvement.

Construction of an AI-centric workforce also involves leveraging cross-functional teams that bring together diverse skill sets and perspectives. AI projects often require collaboration between data scientists, engineers, business analysts, domain experts, and end-users. Cross-functional teams can enhance the quality and effectiveness of AI solutions by integrating different viewpoints and expertise. Leaders should promote a collaborative approach, encouraging open communication and knowledge sharing across departments. Creating structures and processes that facilitate teamwork, such as agile project management frameworks, can help ensure that AI projects are executed efficiently and effectively.

Diversity and inclusion are critical components of an AI-centric workforce. Diverse teams bring a wide range of perspectives and experiences, which can drive innovation and improve decision-making. Organizations should strive to create an inclusive environment where all employees feel valued and empowered to contribute.

Efforts to promote diversity and inclusion should include recruitment strategies that target underrepresented groups, mentorship and sponsorship programs, and initiatives that support career development for diverse employees. By fostering an inclusive culture, organizations can attract and retain a broader range of talent, enhancing their ability to innovate and compete in the AI era. Building an AI-centric workforce requires empowering leaders to guide their teams through the complexities of AI integration. Leaders must be equipped with the skills and knowledge to make informed decisions about AI technologies, manage AI-driven projects, and foster an environment that supports innovation and ethical AI use. Leadership development programs that focus on AI literacy, strategic thinking, and change management can help prepare leaders to navigate the challenges and opportunities of the AI era.

Creating this type of workforce involves attracting and developing AI talent, fostering an AI-ready culture, implementing effective AI governance and risk management frameworks, ensuring continuous education and skill development, leveraging cross-functional teams, promoting diversity and inclusion, and empowering leadership. By taking these steps, organizations can create a workforce that is well-equipped to leverage AI technologies, drive innovation, and achieve sustainable success in a rapidly evolving landscape.

Attracting top AI talent begins with building a strong employer brand that highlights the organization's commitment to innovation, growth, and cutting-edge technologies. Organizations should leverage social media, industry conferences, and networking events to showcase their achievements in AI and their vision for the future. Highlighting successful AI projects, collaborations with leading academic and research institutions, and testimonials from current employees can help create a compelling narrative that attracts top talent. Offering competitive salaries and benefits is essential to attract high-caliber AI professionals. In addition to traditional compensation packages, organizations can offer performance-based incentives, stock options, and bonuses tied to the success of AI initiatives. Benefits such as flexible work arrangements, remote work options, and comprehensive health and wellness programs can also enhance the attractiveness of the organization.

Establishing partnerships with universities, research institutions, and industry groups can help organizations tap into a pool of emerging AI talent. Sponsoring hackathons, AI competitions, and research projects can provide visibility and opportunities to engage with top students and researchers in the field. Offering internships, co-op programs, and apprenticeships can help organizations identify and nurture potential AI talent early. These programs provide valuable hands-on experience for students and young professionals while allowing organizations to evaluate their skills and fit within the company.

Once top AI talent is attracted, it is crucial to invest in their development to ensure they have the skills and knowledge needed to drive innovation and success. A robust onboarding program helps new hires acclimate to the organization's culture, understand their roles, and become productive quickly. This includes training on the organization's AI tools, systems, and processes, as well as introductions to key stakeholders and team members. The rapidly evolving field of AI requires ongoing education and skill development. Organizations should provide access to online courses, workshops, conferences, and certifications in areas such as machine learning, data science, and AI ethics. Encouraging employees to pursue advanced degrees and industry certifications can further enhance their expertise.

Establishing mentorship programs that pair experienced AI professionals with newer employees can facilitate knowledge transfer and professional growth. Creating platforms for knowledge sharing, such as internal forums, lunch-and-learn sessions, and collaborative projects, can also help employees stay updated on the latest AI advancements and best practices. Setting up innovation labs or centers of excellence focused on AI can provide employees with opportunities to work on cutting-edge projects and explore new technologies. Encouraging participation in special projects and cross-functional teams can help employees apply their skills in diverse contexts and drive innovation.

Retaining top AI talent requires creating an environment that supports their professional growth, recognizes their contributions, and fosters a sense of belonging and purpose. Providing clear pathways for career progression is essential for retaining AI talent. Organizations should offer opportunities for lateral moves, promotions, and leadership roles that align with employees' career goals. Regular performance reviews and career development discussions can help employees understand their growth potential and set goals for their future. A positive workplace culture that values diversity, equity, and inclusion can enhance employee satisfaction and retention. Organizations should implement initiatives that promote a sense of belonging, such as employee resource groups, diversity training, and inclusive policies. Encouraging open communication, collaboration, and mutual respect among team members can also create a supportive environment.

Recognizing and rewarding employees' contributions to AI projects can boost morale and motivation. This can include formal recognition programs, such as employee of the month awards, as well as informal acknowledgments, such as shout-outs during team meetings. Providing opportunities for employees to showcase their work to senior leadership and at industry events can also enhance their sense of accomplishment and visibility. AI professionals are often motivated by the opportunity to work on impactful and innovative projects. Organizations should ensure that their AI initiatives align with broader business goals and have the potential to make a significant difference. Providing employees with challenging and meaningful work that allows them to apply their skills and make a tangible impact can enhance job satisfaction and retention. Supporting employees' work-life balance and well-being is crucial for long-term retention. Organizations should offer flexible work arrangements, remote work options, and wellness programs that address physical, mental, and emotional health. Encouraging employees to take time off and providing resources for stress management can help prevent burnout and ensure sustained productivity.

Attracting, developing, and retaining AI talent requires a strategic and holistic approach that addresses the needs and aspirations of AI professionals. By building a strong employer brand, offering competitive compensation and benefits, investing in continuous learning and development, fostering a supportive and inclusive culture, and providing meaningful career advancement opportunities, organizations can create an environment where AI talent thrives. This AI-centric workforce will be well-equipped to drive innovation, enhance operational efficiency, and achieve sustainable success in a rapidly evolving technological landscape.

Investing in AI infrastructure and platforms is crucial for organizations aiming to harness the power of artificial intelligence to drive innovation, improve efficiency, and maintain a competitive edge. A robust AI infrastructure provides the foundation needed to support AI initiatives, from data collection and storage to model development and deployment. This involves not only the physical hardware and software platforms but also the processes and strategies that enable effective AI implementation.

Building a strong AI infrastructure begins with ensuring access to high-quality data. Data is the lifeblood of AI, and having a comprehensive data strategy is essential. Organizations need to invest in data management systems that facilitate the collection, storage, and processing of large volumes of data from diverse sources. This includes implementing data lakes, data warehouses, and cloud storage solutions that provide scalable and secure environments for data storage. Additionally, data governance frameworks must be established to ensure data quality, accuracy, and compliance with regulations such as GDPR.

The computational power required for AI processing necessitates investment in advanced hardware. High-performance computing (HPC) systems, including GPUs and TPUs, are essential for training complex AI models. These specialized processors are optimized for the parallel processing tasks typical in AI and machine learning workloads. Organizations should evaluate their computational needs and invest in the appropriate hardware to support their AI initiatives. For many, this might mean leveraging cloud-based AI platforms, which offer scalable, on-demand resources without the need for significant upfront capital expenditure.

Software platforms and tools are equally important in building an effective AI infrastructure. Organizations should invest in AI and machine learning frameworks such as TensorFlow, PyTorch, and Scikit-learn, which provide the libraries and tools necessary for model development. Integrated development environments (IDEs) and collaborative platforms like Jupyter Notebooks facilitate experimentation and collaboration among data scientists and engineers. These tools streamline the development process, allowing teams to build, test, and refine AI models efficiently.

AI infrastructure also encompasses the deployment and operationalization of AI models. Investing in platforms that support the deployment of AI models into production environments is crucial. This includes machine learning operations (MLOps) platforms that automate the deployment, monitoring, and maintenance of models, ensuring they perform reliably and efficiently. MLOps platforms integrate with existing IT infrastructure and provide tools for version control, model tracking, and automated scaling, facilitating continuous integration and continuous deployment (CI/CD) practices for AI. Security and compliance are critical considerations when investing in AI infrastructure. Organizations must ensure that their AI systems are secure from cyber threats and that data privacy is maintained. This involves implementing robust security measures such as encryption, access controls, and regular security audits. Compliance with data protection regulations and industry standards must be prioritized to avoid legal and reputational risks. Investing in security tools and practices that protect data and AI models from breaches and attacks is essential for maintaining trust and reliability.

Investing in AI infrastructure also requires a focus on sustainability and efficiency. High-performance computing and data storage can consume significant amounts of energy, contributing to the organization's carbon footprint. Organizations should explore energy-efficient hardware options and leverage renewable energy sources where possible. Additionally, optimizing algorithms and models for efficiency can reduce computational requirements and energy consumption. Implementing sustainable practices in AI infrastructure not only supports environmental goals but can also result in cost savings.

Building a skilled workforce is integral to maximizing the value of AI infrastructure investments. Organizations must invest in training and development programs that equip employees with the skills needed to effectively utilize AI tools and platforms. This includes technical training for data scientists, engineers, and IT professionals, as well as education on data governance, security, and ethical AI practices. Encouraging a culture of continuous learning and innovation ensures that the organization remains at the forefront of AI advancements.

Organizations should foster partnerships and collaborations to enhance their AI capabilities. Partnering with technology vendors, academic institutions, and industry consortia can provide access to cutting-edge research, advanced tools, and a broader talent pool. These collaborations can accelerate AI development and deployment, driving innovation and enabling organizations to stay competitive in a rapidly evolving landscape. Investing in AI infrastructure and platforms is essential for organizations seeking to leverage AI for innovation and efficiency. This involves ensuring access to high-quality data, investing in advanced hardware and software, implementing robust security and compliance measures, and focusing on sustainability. Building a skilled workforce and fostering strategic partnerships further enhance the organization's AI capabilities. By making these investments, organizations can create a solid foundation for AI initiatives, driving transformative outcomes and maintaining a competitive edge in the digital age.

Implementing effective AI governance and risk management frameworks is critical for ensuring that AI initiatives are successful, ethical, and sustainable. As AI technologies become more pervasive, organizations must establish robust frameworks that address the ethical, legal, and operational risks associated with AI deployment. These frameworks help mitigate risks, ensure compliance with regulations, and build trust among stakeholders. AI governance involves establishing policies, procedures, and structures that guide the development, deployment, and monitoring of AI systems. The first step in implementing AI governance is defining clear roles and responsibilities. Organizations should designate a governance team that includes representatives from leadership, data science, IT, legal, compliance, and ethics. This team is responsible for overseeing AI initiatives, ensuring that they align with the organization's values and strategic goals.

A comprehensive AI governance framework includes policies that address data privacy, security, and ethical considerations. Data privacy policies should comply with regulations such as GDPR, CCPA, and other relevant laws, ensuring that personal data is collected, processed, and stored responsibly. Security policies must safeguard AI systems from cyber threats, implementing measures such as encryption, access controls, and regular security audits. Ethical policies should address issues such as bias, transparency, and accountability, guiding the ethical design and use of AI systems.

Risk management is an integral part of AI governance. Organizations must identify, assess, and mitigate risks associated with AI deployment. This involves conducting risk assessments to evaluate potential impacts on privacy, security, and ethics. Regular audits and reviews of AI systems help identify vulnerabilities and ensure compliance with governance policies. Implementing a risk management framework that includes risk identification, assessment, mitigation, and monitoring processes ensures that risks are managed proactively.

One critical aspect of AI governance is addressing algorithmic bias. Bias in AI systems can lead to unfair and discriminatory outcomes, undermining trust and credibility. Organizations must implement measures to detect and mitigate bias in AI models. This includes using diverse and representative datasets, applying fairness-aware algorithms, and conducting bias audits. Regularly reviewing and updating models based on feedback and performance data helps ensure that AI systems remain fair and unbiased.

Transparency is another essential component of AI governance. Organizations must ensure that AI systems are transparent and explainable, providing clear insights into how decisions are made. This builds trust among stakeholders and enables accountability. Implementing explainable AI (XAI) techniques helps make complex AI models more interpretable, allowing users to understand the rationale behind AI-driven decisions. Transparent communication about AI policies, practices, and performance further enhances stakeholder confidence. Accountability in AI governance involves establishing mechanisms to hold individuals and teams responsible for AI outcomes. This includes setting up an AI ethics board or committee that oversees AI projects and ensures adherence to ethical guidelines. Creating a feedback loop where employees and stakeholders can raise concerns about AI practices promotes accountability and continuous improvement.

Ensuring that there are clear consequences for violations of AI policies reinforces the importance of ethical behavior.

AI governance frameworks should also include continuous monitoring and evaluation processes. Regularly assessing the performance and impact of AI systems helps identify areas for improvement and ensures that AI initiatives remain aligned with organizational goals. Monitoring key performance indicators (KPIs) related to accuracy, fairness, and efficiency provides insights into the effectiveness of AI systems. Incorporating feedback from users and stakeholders into the evaluation process helps refine AI models and governance practices.

Training and education are vital for effective AI governance. Employees at all levels should be educated about AI policies, ethical considerations, and risk management practices. Providing training programs that cover topics such as data privacy, security, and ethical AI helps build a culture of responsibility and awareness. Encouraging employees to stay updated with the latest developments in AI governance and risk management ensures that the organization remains compliant and proactive in addressing emerging challenges.

Fostering a culture of ethical AI within the organization is essential for successful AI governance. Leaders should promote values such as fairness, transparency, and accountability, setting the tone for ethical behavior. Encouraging open dialogue about ethical dilemmas and creating an environment where employees feel comfortable raising concerns helps build a strong ethical foundation. Recognizing and rewarding ethical behavior reinforces the importance of adhering to AI governance principles.

Implementing effective AI governance and risk management frameworks is crucial for ensuring the ethical and sustainable deployment of AI technologies. This involves defining clear roles and responsibilities, establishing comprehensive policies, conducting risk assessments, and addressing algorithmic bias. Ensuring transparency, accountability, and continuous monitoring further enhances the effectiveness of AI governance. Training and education programs help build a culture of responsibility and awareness, fostering an environment where ethical AI practices are prioritized. By implementing robust governance and risk management frameworks, organizations can mitigate risks, ensure compliance, and build trust among stakeholders, paving the way for successful and responsible AI initiatives.

Part III: Leadership Competencies for the AI Era

As artificial intelligence continues to transform industries and reshape business practices, leaders must develop a new set of competencies to navigate this rapidly evolving landscape. Part III of this book focuses on the critical leadership skills needed to thrive in the AI era, emphasizing the importance of strategic thinking, collaboration, communication, adaptability, and resilience.

Chapter 7 explores the essential components of strategic thinking and vision. Leaders must anticipate and navigate AI-driven disruptions, developing business strategies and models that leverage AI's capabilities. This requires a strategic transformation with a long-term perspective, ensuring that AI is integrated into the core of the business. A clear vision for AI use, effectively communicated to all stakeholders, is vital for successful implementation. Involving stakeholders early in the process helps manage concerns and ensures transparency, fostering a collaborative approach to AI adoption.

Chapter 8 investigates the importance of collaboration and teamwork in the AI era. A supportive corporate culture that encourages participation and allows for mistakes is crucial for AI adoption. Leaders must foster an environment that integrates AI into the leadership process and supports innovation and change. Building cross-functional and interdisciplinary teams is essential for harnessing diverse perspectives and expertise. Facilitating human-AI collaboration and synergy is key to maximizing AI's potential, while promoting trust, transparency, and accountability in AI systems ensures ethical and effective use.

Chapter 9 addresses the critical role of communication and influence in AI-related initiatives. Effective communication strategies are necessary to convey the benefits and implications of AI to all stakeholders. Leaders must influence and inspire their teams, guiding them through the AI journey and addressing any concerns that arise. Building AI literacy across the organization is essential for fostering understanding and acceptance, enabling employees to engage with AI technologies confidently and effectively.

Chapter 10 focuses on the importance of adaptability and resilience in the face of AI-driven change. Embracing change and uncertainty is a fundamental aspect of leadership in the AI era. Leaders must develop resilience and agility to respond to AI-driven disruptions and challenges. Fostering a culture of continuous learning and improvement ensures that the organization remains adaptable and capable of evolving with the technological landscape.

Part III highlights the key leadership competencies required to succeed in the AI era. Strategic thinking, collaboration, communication, adaptability, and resilience are crucial for navigating the complexities of AI integration. By developing these skills, leaders can guide their organizations through the transformative impact of AI, driving innovation and achieving sustainable success.

Chapter 7: Strategic Thinking and Vision

As AI technologies continue to advance, they bring about significant disruptions across various industries. These disruptions can reshape markets, alter competitive dynamics, and change how businesses operate. Anticipating and navigating these AI-driven disruptions is a critical competency for leaders in the AI era. To successfully manage these changes, leaders must stay informed about technological trends, understand the potential impacts of AI on their industry, and develop proactive strategies to adapt and thrive.

One of the key aspects of anticipating AI-driven disruptions is staying informed about the latest advancements in AI technology. This involves continuously monitoring developments in machine learning, natural language processing, computer vision, and other AI-related fields. Leaders should actively engage with academic research, industry reports, and thought leadership to stay ahead of emerging trends. By maintaining a pulse on the technological landscape, leaders can better predict which innovations are likely to impact their industry and prepare accordingly.

Understanding the potential impacts of AI on an industry requires a comprehensive analysis of how AI technologies can transform business processes, customer experiences, and competitive dynamics. Leaders need to identify areas within their organization where AI can drive efficiency, enhance decision-making, and create new value propositions. This might include automating routine tasks, leveraging data analytics for more informed decisions, or developing AI-driven products and services. Assessing these opportunities helps leaders to prioritize AI initiatives that align with their strategic goals.

Developing proactive strategies to adapt to AI-driven disruptions involves several critical steps. First, leaders must foster a culture of innovation within their organization, encouraging experimentation and embracing new ideas. This can be achieved by creating dedicated innovation teams, investing in research and development, and providing resources for pilot projects. Encouraging a mindset of continuous improvement helps the organization to remain agile and responsive to technological changes.

Another important strategy is to invest in reskilling and upskilling the workforce. As AI automates certain tasks and changes the nature of work, employees will need new skills to stay relevant. Leaders should identify the skills gaps within their organization and provide training programs to equip employees with the necessary competencies. This not only helps to mitigate the impact of job displacement but also empowers employees to leverage AI technologies effectively in their roles.

Collaborating with external partners is also essential for navigating AI-driven disruptions. Partnerships with technology vendors, academic institutions, and industry consortia can provide access to cutting-edge AI technologies, research, and expertise. These collaborations can accelerate AI adoption, drive innovation, and enhance the organization's ability to respond to disruptive changes. Leaders should seek out strategic partnerships that align with their AI goals and foster mutually beneficial relationships.

Scenario planning is a valuable tool for anticipating and preparing for AI-driven disruptions. By envisioning different future scenarios and their potential impacts, leaders can develop contingency plans and strategies to address various outcomes. This process involves identifying key uncertainties, exploring their implications, and assessing the organization's readiness to respond. Scenario planning helps leaders to think strategically about the future, make informed decisions, and build resilience against unexpected changes.

Ensuring robust data governance and ethical AI practices is crucial for maintaining trust and credibility during AI-driven disruptions. Leaders must establish policies and frameworks that govern the use of data and AI, addressing issues such as data privacy, security, and algorithmic bias. Transparent communication about AI initiatives and their impacts helps to build trust with stakeholders, including employees, customers, and regulators. Ethical AI practices ensure that AI technologies are used responsibly and for the benefit of all stakeholders.

Anticipating and navigating AI-driven disruptions requires leaders to stay informed about technological advancements, understand the potential impacts of AI on their industry, and develop proactive strategies to adapt and thrive. By fostering a culture of innovation, investing in workforce reskilling, collaborating with external partners, engaging in scenario planning, and ensuring robust data governance, leaders can effectively manage AI-driven changes. These competencies enable organizations to harness the transformative power of AI, drive innovation, and achieve sustainable success in a rapidly evolving landscape.

Developing business strategies and models that leverage AI's transformative potential is crucial for maintaining a competitive edge and driving sustainable growth. AI can revolutionize various aspects of business operations, from optimizing internal processes to creating new revenue streams through innovative products and services. To effectively harness AI, leaders must develop strategies that integrate AI into the core of their business and adapt their models to capitalize on AI-driven opportunities. Developing AI-enabled business strategies begins with a clear understanding of the organization's goals and how AI can support these objectives. Leaders need to identify key areas where AI can add value, such as enhancing customer experiences, improving operational efficiency, or enabling data-driven decision-making. By aligning AI initiatives with strategic priorities, organizations can ensure that AI investments deliver tangible benefits and support long-term growth.

A comprehensive AI strategy should include a detailed assessment of the organization's current capabilities and resources. This involves evaluating the existing data infrastructure, technological tools, and talent pool to identify gaps and areas for improvement. Leaders must prioritize building a robust data foundation, as high-quality data is essential for training accurate and effective AI models. Investing in advanced analytics platforms, cloud computing, and AI development tools can further enhance the organization's AI capabilities.

Collaboration across departments is essential for developing effective AI strategies. Leaders should foster cross-functional teams that bring together diverse expertise from data science, IT, operations, marketing, and other relevant areas. These teams can work together to identify AI use cases, develop pilot projects, and scale successful initiatives across the organization. Encouraging collaboration ensures that AI solutions are well-integrated and aligned with business objectives.

Experimentation is a key component of developing AI-enabled business strategies. Organizations should adopt a mindset of continuous learning and innovation, embracing experimentation and risk-taking. This involves creating a structured approach to pilot AI projects, where teams can test new ideas, measure their impact, and iterate based on feedback. By running small-scale experiments, organizations can validate AI solutions before scaling them, reducing risks and increasing the likelihood of success.

Fostering a culture of innovation and experimentation with AI requires leaders to provide the necessary resources and support. This includes allocating budget for AI research and development, investing in training and development programs, and creating dedicated innovation labs or centers of excellence. These initiatives enable teams to explore cutting-edge AI technologies, develop new applications, and stay ahead of industry trends.

Organizations should also leverage external partnerships to enhance their AI strategies. Collaborating with AI vendors, academic institutions, and industry consortia can provide access to advanced technologies, research insights, and a broader talent pool. These partnerships can accelerate AI adoption, drive innovation, and help organizations stay competitive in a rapidly evolving landscape. Innovation and experimentation are crucial for harnessing the full potential of AI. To foster a culture of innovation, leaders must encourage a mindset that embraces change, values creativity, and rewards experimentation. This involves creating an environment where employees feel empowered to explore new ideas, take calculated risks, and learn from failures.

One effective way to promote innovation is through structured innovation programs and initiatives. Organizations can establish innovation labs or centers of excellence focused on AI, where teams can collaborate on cutting-edge projects and explore new applications of AI technologies. These labs provide a safe space for experimentation, allowing teams to test hypotheses, develop prototypes, and iterate on solutions. Hackathons, innovation challenges, and internal competitions can also stimulate creativity and engagement. By organizing events that encourage employees to come up with innovative AI solutions, organizations can tap into the collective intelligence and diverse perspectives of their workforce. These initiatives foster a sense of excitement and ownership, motivating employees to contribute their best ideas.

Providing access to the latest AI tools and technologies is essential for fostering innovation. Organizations should invest in advanced AI platforms, data analytics tools, and development environments that enable teams to experiment and innovate effectively. Ensuring that employees have the necessary training and support to use these tools is equally important. Continuous learning programs, workshops, and certifications can help employees stay updated with the latest advancements in AI and develop new skills.

Collaboration and knowledge sharing are critical for driving innovation with AI. Leaders should encourage cross-functional teams and interdisciplinary collaboration, bringing together experts from different domains to work on AI projects. This diversity of thought and expertise can lead to more creative and effective solutions. Creating platforms for knowledge sharing, such as internal forums, workshops, and lunch-and-learn sessions, can further enhance collaboration and innovation.

Leaders play a crucial role in fostering a culture of innovation by setting the tone and leading by example. They should communicate a clear vision for AI innovation, highlighting its importance for the organization's future success. Recognizing and celebrating innovative efforts and achievements can also reinforce the value of innovation and motivate employees to continue exploring new ideas.

Developing AI-enabled business strategies and fostering innovation and experimentation with AI are essential for organizations aiming to leverage AI's transformative potential. By aligning AI initiatives with strategic goals, investing in the necessary infrastructure and talent, encouraging collaboration and experimentation, and fostering a culture of continuous learning and innovation, organizations can harness AI to drive sustainable growth and maintain a competitive edge in the AI era.

Implementing AI within an organization necessitates a strategic transformation that is both comprehensive and forward-thinking. This transformation extends beyond the mere adoption of new technologies; it involves reshaping business processes, redefining roles, and fostering a culture that supports continuous innovation and adaptation. A long-term perspective is essential to fully realize the benefits of AI and to ensure that its integration aligns with the organization's strategic goals and values.

At the core of this transformation is the need for a clear and compelling vision for AI. Leaders must articulate how AI will be integrated into the organization's operations, how it will drive value, and how it aligns with the overarching strategic objectives. This vision serves as a guiding star, helping to steer the organization through the complexities of AI adoption and ensuring that all initiatives contribute to a coherent and cohesive strategy.

Developing this vision requires a thorough understanding of AI's potential and its implications for the organization. Leaders must assess how AI can enhance existing processes, create new business models, and deliver superior customer experiences. This involves identifying key areas where AI can drive efficiency, innovation, and competitive advantage. A comprehensive assessment of the current capabilities and resources is also crucial to pinpoint gaps and opportunities for improvement.

Once the vision is established, it is vital to communicate it effectively to all stakeholders. Clear communication helps to build understanding, generate buy-in, and align efforts across the organization. This includes not only internal stakeholders, such as employees and management teams, but also external stakeholders, such as customers, partners, and investors. Engaging stakeholders early in the process helps to address concerns, manage expectations, and foster a sense of shared purpose.

Strategic transformation also requires a robust governance framework to guide AI implementation. This includes establishing policies and standards for data management, algorithm development, and ethical considerations. Effective governance ensures that AI initiatives are conducted responsibly, transparently, and in compliance with regulatory requirements. It also provides a framework for monitoring and evaluating AI projects, ensuring that they deliver the intended outcomes and contribute to the long-term strategic goals.

Investing in the necessary infrastructure is another critical component of AI implementation. This involves building the technological foundation, such as data storage, processing capabilities, and AI development platforms, required to support AI initiatives. High-quality data is essential for training effective AI models, and robust computing resources are necessary for handling the complex algorithms involved in AI applications. Organizations must also invest in tools and technologies that facilitate collaboration, experimentation, and continuous improvement.

A long-term perspective on AI implementation recognizes that the journey is iterative and evolutionary. It requires ongoing investment in talent development, ensuring that employees have the skills and knowledge needed to work effectively with AI technologies. This includes providing training and development opportunities, fostering a culture of continuous learning, and encouraging experimentation and innovation. By cultivating an environment where employees feel empowered to explore and innovate, organizations can stay agile and responsive to technological advancements. Strategic transformation with AI involves rethinking traditional business models and processes. AI can automate routine tasks, provide insights through advanced analytics, and enable new ways of delivering value to customers. Leaders must be willing to challenge the status quo, reengineer processes, and adopt new business models that leverage AI's capabilities. This might include shifting from product-centric to service-centric models, exploring new revenue streams, or creating personalized customer experiences.

A long-term perspective on AI implementation emphasizes sustainability and scalability. AI initiatives should be designed to scale as the organization grows and as technology evolves. This involves building flexible and modular systems that can adapt to changing needs and integrating AI in a way that is sustainable over the long term. Ensuring that AI projects are aligned with strategic priorities and deliver measurable value is essential for maintaining momentum and securing ongoing support from stakeholders. AI implementation requires a strategic transformation that is guided by a clear vision, supported by robust governance, and underpinned by a long-term perspective. By investing in the necessary infrastructure, fostering a culture of continuous learning and innovation, and rethinking traditional business models, organizations can effectively harness the power of AI. This strategic approach enables organizations to navigate the complexities of AI adoption, drive sustainable growth, and maintain a competitive edge in an increasingly AI-driven world.

A clear and compelling vision for the use of AI is essential for leaders to guide their organizations through the complexities and opportunities presented by AI technologies. This vision must articulate how AI will be integrated into the organization's operations, the benefits it will bring, and how it aligns with the organization's strategic objectives and values. Effectively communicating this vision to all stakeholders is crucial for generating buy-in, managing expectations, and fostering a culture of innovation and collaboration.

Having a clear vision for AI use begins with a thorough understanding of the organization's goals and how AI can support these objectives. Leaders must identify the key areas where AI can drive value, whether it's enhancing customer experiences, improving operational efficiency, or enabling data-driven decision-making. This vision should outline the specific AI initiatives that will be pursued, the expected outcomes, and the metrics that will be used to measure success.

Once the vision is established, leaders must communicate it effectively to all stakeholders. This includes not only internal stakeholders such as employees and management teams but also external stakeholders such as customers, partners, and investors. Clear communication helps to build understanding, generate enthusiasm, and align efforts across the organization. Leaders should use a variety of communication channels, such as town hall meetings, newsletters, and digital platforms, to share the vision and provide regular updates on progress.

Effective communication involves more than just sharing information; it also requires engaging stakeholders in meaningful dialogue. Leaders should invite feedback, address concerns, and be transparent about the challenges and uncertainties associated with AI implementation. This open and inclusive approach helps to build trust and ensures that stakeholders feel heard and valued. By involving stakeholders in the conversation, leaders can tap into a diverse range of perspectives and ideas, which can enhance the quality and success of AI initiatives. Involving stakeholders early in the AI implementation process is critical for managing concerns and ensuring transparency. Early engagement helps to identify potential issues, address them proactively, and build a sense of ownership and commitment among stakeholders. It also provides an opportunity to educate stakeholders about AI technologies, their potential impacts, and the steps being taken to ensure responsible and ethical use.

One of the key concerns stakeholders may have is the impact of AI on jobs and job roles. By involving employees early in the process, leaders can provide clarity about how AI will be used to augment rather than replace human capabilities. They can outline plans for reskilling and upskilling employees, ensuring that the workforce is prepared for the changes brought about by AI. Transparent communication about the benefits of AI, such as reducing mundane tasks and freeing up time for more strategic work, can help alleviate fears and build support for AI initiatives.

Involving stakeholders early also helps to ensure that AI initiatives are aligned with the needs and expectations of those who will be affected by them. For example, engaging with customers can provide valuable insights into their preferences and pain points, which can inform the design and development of AI-driven products and services. Similarly, collaborating with partners and suppliers can help to identify opportunities for joint innovation and ensure that AI solutions are compatible with broader ecosystem requirements.

Transparency is a cornerstone of effective stakeholder engagement. Leaders must be open about the goals, processes, and potential risks associated with AI implementation. This includes being honest about the limitations of AI technologies and the uncertainties involved in their deployment. Providing regular updates on progress, sharing successes and setbacks, and being responsive to stakeholder feedback are all essential for maintaining trust and credibility. Transparency also extends to ethical considerations. Stakeholders are increasingly concerned about the ethical implications of AI, such as privacy, bias, and accountability. Leaders must address these concerns by establishing clear ethical guidelines for AI use and demonstrating a commitment to responsible AI practices. This might include implementing robust data governance frameworks, conducting regular audits of AI systems for bias and fairness, and ensuring compliance with relevant regulations and standards. A clear vision for AI use, effectively communicated to all stakeholders, is essential for guiding successful AI implementation. Involving stakeholders early in the process helps to manage concerns, ensure transparency, and build a collaborative and supportive environment. By fostering open dialogue, providing education and support, and demonstrating a commitment to ethical AI practices, leaders can build trust and drive the successful adoption of AI technologies. This strategic approach enables organizations to harness the transformative power of AI, driving innovation and achieving sustainable success in an increasingly AI-driven world.

Chapter 8: Collaboration and Teamwork

Adopting artificial intelligence within an organization is not merely a technological endeavor; it necessitates a fundamental shift in corporate culture. A supportive corporate culture is crucial for AI adoption, as it encourages participation from all levels of the organization and allows for mistakes, fostering an environment where innovation can thrive.

A supportive corporate culture begins with leadership. Leaders must champion AI initiatives, demonstrating their commitment to the technology and its potential to transform the organization. This involves not only advocating for AI but also setting an example by being open to learning and experimentation. When leaders are visibly engaged in AI projects and show a willingness to embrace new ideas and approaches, it sets a tone that encourages the entire organization to follow suit.

Encouraging participation from all levels of the organization is essential for successful AI adoption. This means creating opportunities for employees to contribute to AI initiatives, regardless of their role or department. Cross-functional teams can be particularly effective, bringing together diverse perspectives and expertise to work on AI projects. Encouraging collaboration between data scientists, engineers, business analysts, and domain experts ensures that AI solutions are well-rounded and address real business needs.

For participation to be meaningful, employees must feel empowered to share their ideas and insights. This requires an environment of psychological safety, where individuals feel comfortable taking risks and expressing their thoughts without fear of criticism or retribution. Leaders can foster psychological safety by actively listening to employees, valuing their contributions, and responding constructively to their input. Recognizing and rewarding participation can further motivate employees to engage with AI initiatives.

Allowing for mistakes is another critical component of a supportive corporate culture. Innovation inherently involves risk, and not all experiments will succeed. An organization that punishes failure stifles creativity and discourages employees from trying new approaches. Instead, leaders should adopt a mindset that views mistakes as learning opportunities. When an AI project does not go as planned, it is important to analyze what went wrong, extract lessons, and apply these insights to future efforts. This iterative process of trial and error is fundamental to innovation and continuous improvement.

To cultivate a culture that embraces experimentation and learning, organizations should establish structured processes for pilot projects and experimentation. These processes should include mechanisms for testing new ideas on a small scale, gathering feedback, and iterating based on the results. By providing a clear framework for experimentation, organizations can manage risk while still encouraging creativity and innovation. Training and education are also vital for building a supportive culture for AI adoption. Employees need to understand what AI is, how it works, and the potential benefits and challenges associated with its use. Providing comprehensive training programs that cover the basics of AI, as well as more advanced topics relevant to specific roles, can help demystify the technology and build confidence in its application. Ongoing education ensures that employees stay up-to-date with the latest developments in AI and continue to build their skills.

Another important aspect of a supportive corporate culture is promoting a mindset of continuous improvement. AI technologies and applications are constantly evolving, and organizations must be willing to adapt and evolve along with them. This requires a commitment to continuous learning and development, both at the individual and organizational levels. Encouraging employees to pursue professional development opportunities, attend conferences, and participate in AI-related communities can help keep the organization at the forefront of technological advancements.

Transparency and open communication are key to maintaining a supportive culture for AI adoption. Leaders should be transparent about the goals, progress, and challenges of AI initiatives. Regular updates and open forums for discussion help keep employees informed and engaged. Addressing concerns and questions openly fosters trust and ensures that employees feel involved in the AI journey. A supportive corporate culture is crucial for AI adoption. By encouraging participation, allowing for mistakes, and fostering an environment of psychological safety, organizations can create a culture where innovation thrives. Leadership plays a pivotal role in setting the tone, advocating for AI, and modeling a willingness to learn and experiment. Training, education, and continuous improvement are essential for building confidence and competence in AI. Transparency and open communication help maintain trust and engagement throughout the organization. By cultivating this supportive culture, organizations can effectively leverage AI to drive innovation, improve efficiency, and achieve long-term success in an increasingly AI-driven world.

The role of leadership extends beyond the traditional scope of guiding teams and making strategic decisions. Leaders must actively foster a culture that integrates AI into the leadership process and supports innovation and change. This involves creating an environment where AI is not only accepted but embraced as a critical tool for driving organizational growth and transformation. To integrate AI into the leadership process, leaders need to exemplify an openness to AI technologies and a willingness to incorporate data-driven insights into their decision-making. This starts with leaders themselves becoming well-versed in AI concepts and understanding how AI can be applied to their specific business contexts. Leaders should prioritize continuous learning and demonstrate their commitment to AI by engaging in training programs, attending AI-focused conferences, and staying updated on the latest AI advancements.

Creating a culture that supports AI integration involves promoting a mindset of curiosity and experimentation across the organization. Leaders should encourage teams to explore new AI applications and to pilot projects that can provide valuable insights and potential competitive advantages. This requires establishing processes that support iterative testing and learning, where teams can experiment with AI solutions on a small scale, gather feedback, and refine their approaches based on results. Celebrating both successes and failures as learning opportunities reinforces the importance of experimentation and reduces the fear of failure.

Communication is a key element in fostering a culture that embraces AI. Leaders must articulate a clear vision for how AI will be used within the organization, outlining the benefits it will bring and how it aligns with the company's strategic goals. Transparent communication helps demystify AI, address any misconceptions, and build trust among employees. Regular updates on AI initiatives, open forums for discussion, and opportunities for employees to ask questions and provide input can further enhance engagement and support for AI adoption.

Empowering employees is crucial for integrating AI into the organizational culture. Leaders should provide access to the necessary tools, resources, and training to enable employees to work effectively with AI technologies. This includes offering comprehensive training programs that cover both the technical aspects of AI and its practical applications within the organization. By equipping employees with the skills and knowledge they need, leaders can foster a sense of ownership and confidence in using AI to enhance their work.

Collaboration is another essential component of a culture that integrates AI. Leaders should encourage cross-functional and interdisciplinary teamwork, bringing together diverse expertise to solve complex problems and develop innovative AI solutions. This collaborative approach not only leverages the strengths of different departments but also fosters a culture of shared learning and mutual support. Creating platforms for knowledge sharing, such as internal forums, workshops, and collaborative projects, can further enhance the integration of AI into the organization.

Leaders must also focus on the ethical implications of AI and ensure that AI technologies are used responsibly. Establishing clear ethical guidelines and governance frameworks for AI use is critical. This includes addressing issues such as data privacy, algorithmic bias, and transparency. By demonstrating a commitment to ethical AI practices, leaders can build trust and credibility with both employees and external stakeholders. Encouraging an open dialogue about the ethical challenges and implications of AI helps to create a culture of accountability and responsible innovation.

Supporting innovation and change requires leaders to be champions of continuous improvement. AI technologies and applications are constantly evolving, and organizations must be willing to adapt and innovate continuously. Leaders should foster a mindset of lifelong learning, encouraging employees to pursue professional development opportunities, stay updated on AI advancements, and explore new ways to apply AI to their work. Recognizing and rewarding innovative efforts can further motivate employees to embrace change and contribute to the organization's AI journey.

Leaders play a pivotal role in fostering a culture that integrates AI into the leadership process and supports innovation and change. This involves exemplifying an openness to AI, promoting a mindset of curiosity and experimentation, and providing clear communication about AI initiatives. Empowering employees with the necessary tools and training, encouraging collaboration, and ensuring ethical AI practices are all critical components of this cultural shift. By championing continuous improvement and fostering an environment that embraces AI, leaders can drive transformative change, enhance organizational performance, and achieve sustainable success in the AI-driven world.

Building cross-functional and interdisciplinary teams is essential for leveraging the full potential of AI technologies within an organization. These teams bring together diverse skills and perspectives, enabling more comprehensive and innovative solutions to complex problems. Cross-functional collaboration fosters a culture of shared learning and mutual support, which is crucial for the successful integration of AI.

The first step is to identify the core competencies and roles needed for AI projects. These typically include data scientists, machine learning engineers, software developers, domain experts, business analysts, and project managers. Each team member brings unique expertise that is essential for the different stages of AI development, from data collection and preprocessing to model building and deployment.

AI projects often require input from various departments, such as IT, operations, marketing, and customer service. Leaders should encourage collaboration across these departments to ensure that AI solutions are aligned with business needs and objectives. Establishing regular inter-departmental meetings and collaborative platforms can facilitate communication and idea sharing.

For cross-functional teams to thrive, leaders must create an environment that encourages open communication and collaboration. This involves providing the necessary tools and platforms for teamwork, such as project management software, collaborative workspaces, and communication tools. Ensuring that team members have access to shared resources and data is also crucial for effective collaboration.

Setting clear goals and objectives for AI projects helps align the efforts of cross-functional teams. Leaders should articulate the specific outcomes they expect from AI initiatives, such as improving operational efficiency, enhancing customer experiences, or driving revenue growth. Clearly defined goals provide a common purpose and direction for the team, fostering unity and focus.

Cross-functional teams benefit from the diverse knowledge and perspectives of their members. Leaders should encourage knowledge sharing through regular meetings, workshops, and training sessions. Creating opportunities for team members to present their work, share insights, and learn from each other enhances the collective expertise of the team and drives innovation.

Innovation in AI often involves experimentation and iteration. Leaders should promote a culture where team members feel empowered to experiment with new ideas, test hypotheses, and learn from failures. Providing a safe space for experimentation, where mistakes are viewed as learning opportunities, encourages creativity and risk-taking.

Agile methodologies, such as Scrum or Kanban, can be highly effective for managing AI projects. These frameworks promote iterative development, continuous feedback, and adaptive planning, which are well-suited to the dynamic nature of AI work. Implementing agile practices helps cross-functional teams stay flexible, respond quickly to changes, and deliver incremental value throughout the project lifecycle.

Strong leadership support is critical for the success of cross-functional AI teams. Leaders should provide guidance, resources, and support to help teams overcome challenges and stay on track. This includes securing necessary funding, removing organizational barriers, and championing the team's efforts to stakeholders. Regular check-ins and progress reviews help ensure that the team is aligned with strategic objectives and making steady progress. A diverse team brings varied perspectives that can lead to more innovative solutions. Leaders should strive to build teams that include a mix of genders, ethnicities, backgrounds, and experiences. Inclusion is equally important; every team member should feel valued and empowered to contribute. Diversity and inclusion can drive creativity and ensure that AI solutions are more comprehensive and free from bias.

To maintain motivation and momentum, it is important to measure the success of AI projects and celebrate achievements. Leaders should establish metrics to evaluate the impact of AI initiatives and recognize the contributions of team members. Celebrating successes, both big and small, reinforces the value of the team's work and encourages continued collaboration and innovation.

Building cross-functional and interdisciplinary teams for AI is essential for leveraging the full potential of AI technologies. By identifying core competencies, fostering collaboration, creating a supportive environment, setting clear goals, encouraging knowledge sharing, promoting experimentation, implementing agile methodologies, ensuring leadership support, embracing diversity and inclusion, and measuring success, leaders can create high-performing teams that drive AI innovation and deliver significant value to the organization. This collaborative approach ensures that AI initiatives are well-rounded, effective, and aligned with the strategic goals of the organization, ultimately leading to sustainable success in the AI era.

Facilitating effective human-AI collaboration and synergy is essential for organizations seeking to maximize the potential of AI technologies. This involves integrating AI tools and systems in a way that enhances human capabilities, fosters seamless interaction, and drives innovative outcomes. Achieving this synergy requires thoughtful planning, a focus on user experience, and ongoing support and training.

Successful human-AI collaboration begins with designing AI systems that are intuitive and user-friendly. AI tools should be developed with the end-users in mind, ensuring that they complement human work processes and are easy to interact with. This involves incorporating user feedback during the development process, conducting usability testing, and making iterative improvements based on user experiences. By focusing on human-centric design principles, organizations can create AI systems that are more likely to be adopted and effectively used by employees.

One of the key benefits of AI is its ability to process vast amounts of data and provide actionable insights. AI can enhance human decision-making by offering data-driven recommendations and identifying patterns that might be missed by human analysis. To facilitate this, AI systems should present information in a clear and understandable manner, providing context and explanations for their recommendations. This transparency helps build trust in AI-driven insights and empowers employees to make informed decisions.

For human-AI collaboration to be effective, employees need to be equipped with the necessary skills and knowledge to work alongside AI systems. Organizations should invest in comprehensive training programs that cover both the technical aspects of AI and its practical applications within the workplace. This includes educating employees on how AI works, its capabilities and limitations, and how to interpret and act on AI-generated insights. Continuous learning opportunities, such as workshops, webinars, and online courses, can help employees stay updated on the latest AI developments and best practices.

Integrating AI into existing workflows requires careful planning and coordination. Leaders should identify tasks and processes where AI can add the most value and redesign workflows to incorporate AI tools seamlessly. This might involve automating routine tasks, augmenting complex decision-making processes, or providing real-time analytics to support strategic planning. By creating collaborative workflows, organizations can ensure that AI systems enhance rather than disrupt human work. Human-AI collaboration is an evolving process, and continuous improvement is key to its success. Organizations should encourage employees to experiment with AI tools and provide feedback on their experiences. This feedback is invaluable for identifying areas where AI systems can be improved and for making adjustments that enhance their usability and effectiveness. Creating a culture of open communication and iterative development helps ensure that AI tools remain aligned with user needs and organizational goals.

Trust is a critical component of effective human-AI collaboration. Employees need to trust that AI systems are reliable, unbiased, and working in their best interests. Organizations can build this trust by ensuring transparency in how AI systems operate and how decisions are made. This involves providing clear explanations for AI-driven recommendations, being open about the data and algorithms used, and addressing any concerns about bias or fairness. By fostering a transparent and ethical approach to AI, organizations can build confidence in AI systems and encourage their effective use.

AI should be seen as a tool that empowers employees, rather than a replacement for human skills. Leaders should emphasize the value of human judgment, creativity, and emotional intelligence, and highlight how AI can enhance these capabilities. By framing AI as a collaborative partner, organizations can help employees see the benefits of AI and encourage them to embrace its use. Empowering employees to take ownership of AI initiatives and to explore new ways of leveraging AI can drive innovation and improve overall performance.

Ethical considerations are paramount in human-AI collaboration. Organizations must establish clear guidelines and governance frameworks to ensure that AI is used responsibly and ethically. This includes addressing issues such as data privacy, algorithmic bias, and the impact of AI on employment. By committing to ethical AI practices, organizations can build trust with employees and stakeholders and ensure that AI technologies are used in ways that align with organizational values and societal expectations.

Creating a culture that supports human-AI collaboration requires leadership commitment and organizational alignment. Leaders should promote a vision of AI that emphasizes collaboration, innovation, and continuous learning. Recognizing and rewarding collaborative efforts, celebrating successes, and sharing stories of successful human-AI partnerships can reinforce the desired culture and motivate employees to engage with AI initiatives.

Facilitating human-AI collaboration and synergy involves designing user-friendly AI systems, enhancing decision-making, providing comprehensive training, creating collaborative workflows, encouraging experimentation and feedback, building trust and transparency, empowering employees, ensuring ethical use of AI, and fostering a collaborative culture. By integrating AI in a way that enhances human capabilities and supports organizational goals, leaders can drive innovation, improve efficiency, and achieve sustainable success in the AI era. This collaborative approach ensures that AI technologies are leveraged effectively, leading to better outcomes for both the organization and its employees.

Promoting trust, transparency, and accountability in AI systems is essential for ensuring their effective and ethical use. Trust in AI systems begins with transparency. Organizations must be open about how AI systems are developed, how they operate, and the data they use. This involves providing clear and understandable explanations of AI models and the rationale behind their decisions. Transparency helps demystify AI, making it more accessible and less intimidating for users. When employees and stakeholders understand how AI systems work, they are more likely to trust and embrace them.

To build transparency, organizations should document AI processes thoroughly, including data sources, model development, and validation procedures. This documentation should be accessible to all relevant stakeholders, allowing them to review and understand the steps taken to ensure the system's reliability and fairness. Regular audits of AI systems can further enhance transparency by providing independent verification of their performance and adherence to ethical standards. These audits can identify potential biases, inaccuracies, and other issues that may undermine trust in AI systems.

Accountability in AI systems means that organizations and individuals must be responsible for the outcomes generated by these technologies. Establishing clear governance structures and roles is crucial for accountability. Organizations should designate specific teams or individuals responsible for overseeing AI initiatives, ensuring they are developed and deployed responsibly. This includes setting up an AI ethics board or committee that can provide guidance on ethical issues, review AI projects, and make recommendations to mitigate potential risks.

Organizations must also implement mechanisms for monitoring AI systems in real-time to ensure they continue to perform as expected and to identify any deviations that may occur. Continuous monitoring allows for prompt corrective actions when issues arise, maintaining the integrity and reliability of AI systems. Additionally, having a robust feedback loop where users can report problems or concerns with AI systems enhances accountability. By actively seeking and addressing user feedback, organizations can improve AI systems and build trust with their users.

Ethical considerations are paramount in promoting trust and accountability. Organizations should establish and adhere to ethical guidelines that govern the use of AI. These guidelines should cover data privacy, consent, and the fair and unbiased application of AI technologies. Ensuring that AI systems do not perpetuate or amplify existing biases is critical. This requires rigorous testing and validation during the development phase, using diverse and representative datasets. Regularly updating AI models to reflect new data and societal changes helps maintain their relevance and fairness. Education and training also play a significant role in promoting trust and accountability. Employees and stakeholders need to be educated about AI, including its capabilities, limitations, and ethical implications. Providing training on how to use AI responsibly and understand its outputs can empower users to make informed decisions. Transparent communication about the potential risks and benefits of AI helps set realistic expectations and fosters a culture of accountability.

Organizations should be proactive in addressing any concerns or issues related to AI systems. This involves being transparent about any limitations or uncertainties in AI models and being prepared to explain and justify decisions made by AI. In cases where AI decisions have significant impacts on individuals or groups, it is essential to have mechanisms for human oversight and appeal. This ensures that affected parties can challenge and seek redress for decisions they believe are unfair or incorrect.

By promoting trust, transparency, and accountability in AI systems, organizations can foster a positive relationship with AI technologies and their users. Transparent practices build confidence, accountability ensures responsible use, and a strong ethical framework guides AI deployment. Together, these elements create an environment where AI can be leveraged effectively and ethically, driving innovation and achieving organizational goals while maintaining public trust and support.

Chapter 9: Communication and Influence

Effective communication strategies for AI-related initiatives are crucial for ensuring that all stakeholders understand the benefits, risks, and implications of AI integration. Clear, consistent, and transparent communication helps build trust, address concerns, and foster a collaborative environment. Leaders should start by articulating a clear vision for AI, explaining how it aligns with the organization's strategic goals and the expected outcomes. This vision should be communicated across various channels, including town hall meetings, newsletters, and digital platforms, to ensure it reaches all employees and stakeholders.

Engaging storytelling is a powerful tool for communicating the potential of AI. By sharing success stories and real-life examples of how AI has positively impacted other organizations or industries, leaders can illustrate the tangible benefits of AI and inspire confidence in its adoption. Highlighting case studies that demonstrate successful AI applications can make the technology more relatable and easier to understand.

Open forums and interactive sessions are essential for addressing questions and concerns about AI. Providing opportunities for employees and stakeholders to ask questions, share their thoughts, and express their concerns fosters an inclusive and transparent culture. Leaders should be prepared to address these questions honestly, acknowledging any limitations or challenges associated with AI. Regular Q&A sessions, workshops, and panel discussions can facilitate this two-way communication and help demystify AI.

Visual aids and simplified explanations can enhance understanding of complex AI concepts. Using infographics, diagrams, and videos to explain how AI works and its potential applications can make the information more accessible. Breaking down technical jargon into simple, clear language ensures that everyone, regardless of their technical background, can grasp the key points.

Regular updates on AI initiatives help maintain engagement and transparency. Leaders should provide ongoing updates on the progress of AI projects, including milestones achieved, challenges encountered, and future plans. These updates can be shared through various internal communication channels, such as intranet portals, email newsletters, and team meetings. Keeping stakeholders informed about the AI journey reinforces trust and demonstrates a commitment to transparency.

Training and education programs are vital for building AI literacy across the organization. Offering workshops, webinars, and online courses on AI basics, ethical considerations, and practical applications can empower employees to understand and engage with AI technologies. Providing resources for self-paced learning and creating a library of AI-related materials can support continuous education and development.

Inclusive communication ensures that all voices are heard and considered. Encouraging diverse perspectives and involving a wide range of stakeholders in discussions about AI can lead to more comprehensive and effective solutions. Creating inclusive platforms for feedback and collaboration, such as suggestion boxes, online forums, and diversity councils, can help capture the diverse insights and concerns of the workforce.

Leaders should also communicate the ethical framework guiding AI use within the organization. Clearly outlining the principles and policies that govern AI deployment, such as data privacy, fairness, and accountability, helps build trust and ensures that AI is used responsibly. Being transparent about the ethical considerations and safeguards in place reassures stakeholders that the organization is committed to ethical AI practices.

Celebrating milestones and achievements in AI projects can boost morale and reinforce the positive impact of AI. Recognizing and rewarding the contributions of teams and individuals involved in AI initiatives can motivate employees and encourage continued engagement. Sharing these successes through internal and external communication channels highlights the organization's progress and commitment to innovation. Effective communication strategies for AI-related initiatives involve clear vision articulation, engaging storytelling, open forums for discussion, visual aids for simplification, regular updates, training and education programs, inclusive communication, transparency about ethical frameworks, and celebrating achievements. By employing these strategies, leaders can foster a culture of trust, transparency, and collaboration, ensuring successful AI integration and driving organizational growth and innovation.

Influencing and inspiring stakeholders in the AI journey requires leaders to effectively communicate the transformative potential of AI and how it aligns with the organization's vision and goals. This starts with articulating a clear and compelling narrative about the role of AI in driving innovation, efficiency, and competitive advantage. Leaders should emphasize the strategic importance of AI, explaining how it will impact various aspects of the business and contribute to long-term success.

Engaging storytelling plays a crucial role in inspiring stakeholders. Sharing success stories and real-world examples of AI applications can illustrate the tangible benefits and positive outcomes AI can bring. By highlighting case studies of organizations that have successfully implemented AI to solve complex problems or create new opportunities, leaders can make the technology more relatable and its potential more apparent. Building trust is essential for gaining stakeholder buy-in. Leaders should be transparent about the AI initiatives, including the goals, challenges, and expected outcomes. Providing regular updates on the progress of AI projects helps maintain transparency and keeps stakeholders informed. Addressing concerns openly and honestly, and showing a willingness to listen to feedback, fosters a sense of collaboration and trust.

Involvement and engagement are key to inspiring stakeholders. Inviting stakeholders to participate in AI projects, from brainstorming sessions to pilot programs, helps them feel more invested in the initiatives. This involvement not only provides valuable insights and diverse perspectives but also builds a sense of ownership and commitment to the success of AI projects.

Education and awareness are critical components of influencing stakeholders. Providing comprehensive training and resources on AI helps demystify the technology and build confidence in its use. Offering workshops, seminars, and access to online courses allows stakeholders to deepen their understanding of AI and its potential applications. This knowledge empowers them to make informed decisions and advocate for AI initiatives within their areas of influence.

Highlighting the ethical considerations and safeguards in place for AI use can also inspire confidence among stakeholders. Clearly communicating the organization's commitment to responsible AI practices, including data privacy, fairness, and accountability, reassures stakeholders that ethical implications are being thoughtfully addressed. This transparency about ethical standards helps build trust and support for AI initiatives. Celebrating successes and recognizing contributions is important for maintaining momentum and enthusiasm. Acknowledging the efforts and achievements of teams and individuals involved in AI projects reinforces the value of their work and motivates continued engagement. Sharing these successes through internal communications and public channels not only boosts morale but also showcases the organization's progress and commitment to innovation.

Leadership by example is powerful in inspiring stakeholders. When leaders themselves are enthusiastic and knowledgeable about AI, it sets a tone that encourages others to follow suit. Demonstrating a willingness to embrace AI, take risks, and learn from both successes and failures shows a commitment to innovation and continuous improvement. Leaders who actively participate in AI initiatives and promote a culture of experimentation and learning can significantly influence and inspire their teams.

Creating a vision that connects AI initiatives to broader organizational goals and societal impacts can further inspire stakeholders. By framing AI projects within the context of how they contribute to the company's mission and positively impact customers, employees, and communities, leaders can create a compelling narrative that resonates on a deeper level. This vision helps stakeholders see the bigger picture and understand the meaningful contributions AI can make.

Influencing and inspiring stakeholders in the AI journey involves clear and compelling communication, engaging storytelling, building trust, involving stakeholders, providing education and resources, highlighting ethical standards, celebrating successes, leading by example, and connecting AI initiatives to broader organizational and societal goals. By employing these strategies, leaders can create a supportive and enthusiastic environment for AI adoption, driving innovation and achieving long-term success.

Building AI literacy across the organization is essential for effectively integrating AI technologies and maximizing their potential. To achieve this, leaders must create a comprehensive and inclusive approach that involves education, engagement, and continuous learning. The first step is to demystify AI by explaining its fundamental concepts in accessible terms. This helps employees understand what AI is, how it works, and its potential applications. Using clear and simple language avoids technical jargon and makes the subject approachable for everyone.

Providing tailored training programs is crucial for enhancing AI literacy. These programs should be designed to meet the needs of different roles within the organization, from basic AI awareness sessions for all employees to more advanced courses for technical staff. Offering workshops, webinars, and online courses allows employees to learn at their own pace and according to their interests and job requirements. Incorporating real-world examples and case studies into these training sessions helps illustrate the practical applications of AI and how it can solve specific business problems.

Engaging employees through hands-on experience is another effective way to build AI literacy. Encouraging participation in pilot projects, hackathons, and innovation labs gives employees the opportunity to work directly with AI tools and technologies. This hands-on approach not only enhances understanding but also fosters a culture of experimentation and innovation. Providing access to AI platforms and resources, such as data sets and development environments, empowers employees to explore and experiment with AI solutions.

Creating a knowledge-sharing culture within the organization further supports AI literacy. Establishing internal forums, discussion groups, and collaborative platforms allows employees to share their experiences, insights, and best practices. Regular knowledge-sharing sessions, such as lunch-and-learns or tech talks, can facilitate the exchange of ideas and promote continuous learning. Encouraging employees to present their AI projects and findings to their peers helps build confidence and reinforces a sense of community.

Leadership plays a vital role in promoting AI literacy. Leaders should model a commitment to learning by participating in AI training programs and staying informed about AI advancements. Their visible support for AI initiatives sends a strong message about the importance of AI literacy. Leaders can also champion AI by integrating it into the organization's strategic vision and goals, making it clear that AI is a priority for future growth and success.

Building partnerships with external experts and institutions can enhance AI literacy efforts. Collaborating with universities, research organizations, and AI vendors can provide access to cutting-edge knowledge and resources. These partnerships can offer additional training opportunities, guest lectures, and access to specialized expertise that may not be available internally.

Ensuring that AI literacy efforts are ongoing and evolving is crucial. AI technologies and applications are continuously advancing, and the organization must keep pace with these changes. Regularly updating training materials, introducing new learning modules, and staying current with industry trends help maintain the relevance and effectiveness of AI literacy programs. Encouraging a mindset of lifelong learning and adaptability prepares employees to navigate the dynamic landscape of AI.

Recognizing and celebrating achievements in AI literacy can motivate employees and reinforce the importance of these efforts. Acknowledging those who have completed training programs, contributed to AI projects, or demonstrated exceptional AI understanding can inspire others to engage with AI learning initiatives. Highlighting success stories and showcasing how AI literacy has positively impacted the organization can further underscore its value. Building AI literacy across the organization involves demystifying AI concepts, providing tailored training programs, engaging employees through hands-on experience, fostering a knowledge-sharing culture, modeling leadership support, leveraging external partnerships, ensuring ongoing learning, and recognizing achievements. By implementing these strategies, organizations can enhance their AI capabilities, foster a culture of innovation, and ensure that employees are equipped to leverage AI technologies effectively, driving long-term success and growth.

Addressing concerns in AI across the organization is essential to foster trust and acceptance. The first step is to create an open and transparent dialogue about AI, where employees feel comfortable expressing their fears and uncertainties. This involves holding town hall meetings, Q&A sessions, and workshops where leaders can listen to concerns and provide clear, honest answers. Transparency about AI projects, including their goals, processes, and potential impacts, helps demystify the technology and build trust.

Educational initiatives are crucial in alleviating concerns. Providing comprehensive training that explains how AI works, its capabilities, and its limitations can reduce fear and misinformation. When employees understand the basics of AI, they are less likely to view it as a mysterious or threatening force. Training should also address the ethical implications of AI, including data privacy, bias, and accountability, to reassure employees that the organization is committed to responsible AI use.

Involving employees in the AI journey can significantly mitigate concerns. By including them in discussions about AI strategy and implementation, organizations can ensure that their voices are heard and their insights are valued. This participatory approach helps build a sense of ownership and reduces resistance to change. Creating cross-functional teams that include employees from various departments encourages collaboration and shows that AI initiatives are inclusive and transparent.

Clear communication about the role of AI in the organization is essential. Leaders must articulate that AI is intended to augment human capabilities, not replace them. Highlighting examples where AI has been used to support employees, enhance their work, and create new opportunities can help shift perceptions. Providing case studies and real-life examples of successful AI implementation can illustrate the positive impact of AI on jobs and business processes. Addressing job security concerns directly is vital. Organizations should communicate plans for reskilling and upskilling employees to prepare them for the changes brought about by AI. Offering training programs, career development opportunities, and pathways for transition can reassure employees that they are valued and their careers are being safeguarded. Emphasizing the organization's commitment to workforce development and continuous learning can alleviate fears about job displacement.

Regular feedback mechanisms are important for addressing ongoing concerns. Establishing channels through which employees can provide feedback on AI projects and their experiences helps identify issues early and allows for timely interventions. This feedback loop demonstrates that the organization values employee input and is committed to making improvements based on their concerns.

Promoting ethical standards and governance in AI use is crucial for building trust. Organizations should establish clear policies and frameworks to ensure that AI is used responsibly and ethically. This includes addressing issues such as data privacy, algorithmic bias, and transparency. Being transparent about these policies and actively demonstrating their implementation reassures employees that the organization is committed to ethical AI practices.

Leaders play a pivotal role in addressing concerns by modeling a positive attitude toward AI and showing empathy toward employees' worries. By being approachable and open to discussions about AI, leaders can create a supportive environment where concerns are addressed constructively. Leadership endorsement of AI initiatives and ethical practices reinforces their importance and encourages acceptance throughout the organization. Celebrating successes and acknowledging contributions related to AI can help shift the narrative from fear to opportunity. Recognizing teams and individuals who have successfully integrated AI into their work, and sharing stories of how AI has positively impacted the organization, can inspire confidence and excitement. Highlighting these achievements publicly reinforces the message that AI can be a powerful tool for innovation and improvement.

Addressing concerns in AI across the organization requires open dialogue, comprehensive education, employee involvement, clear communication, reassurance about job security, regular feedback mechanisms, ethical governance, and strong leadership. By fostering an environment of transparency, inclusion, and continuous learning, organizations can build trust in AI technologies and ensure their successful integration into business processes.

Chapter 10: Adaptability and Resilience

Embracing change and uncertainty in the AI era is crucial for organizations aiming to thrive in a rapidly evolving technological landscape. Leaders must cultivate a mindset that views change as an opportunity for growth and innovation rather than a threat. This involves fostering a culture of agility and resilience where employees are encouraged to adapt quickly to new developments and embrace continuous learning.

Effective communication is key to managing change and uncertainty. Leaders should consistently articulate the vision for AI integration and the strategic benefits it brings. Transparent communication about the changes AI will bring, both in the short term and long term, helps reduce anxiety and builds trust. Explaining the reasons behind AI initiatives and how they align with the organization's goals can create a shared sense of purpose and direction.

Supporting employees through change requires providing the necessary tools and resources. Offering training and development programs helps employees build the skills needed to work effectively with AI technologies. Encouraging a growth mindset, where challenges are viewed as opportunities to learn and improve, can motivate employees to embrace new roles and responsibilities that AI might introduce.

Creating a supportive environment where experimentation and risk-taking are encouraged is essential. Organizations should allow room for trial and error, recognizing that not all AI projects will succeed on the first attempt. Learning from failures and iterating on solutions fosters innovation and resilience. Leaders should celebrate both successes and the lessons learned from unsuccessful attempts, reinforcing the value of continuous improvement.

Involving employees in the AI journey helps them feel more connected to the changes occurring. Soliciting their input and feedback on AI projects and implementation strategies ensures that diverse perspectives are considered. This participatory approach can also uncover potential issues early, allowing for proactive adjustments and fostering a sense of ownership and collaboration.

Developing robust change management strategies is crucial for navigating uncertainty. This includes setting clear objectives, timelines, and metrics for AI initiatives. Regularly reviewing progress and being flexible enough to adjust plans based on new information or challenges ensures that the organization remains responsive and adaptive. Leaders should provide guidance and support to teams as they navigate the complexities of AI integration, helping them stay focused and aligned with strategic goals.

Fostering a culture of resilience involves encouraging employees to develop skills that enhance their adaptability and problem-solving abilities. This can be achieved through workshops, coaching, and mentoring programs that focus on building resilience and agility. Recognizing and rewarding resilience in the face of change reinforces its importance and motivates employees to develop these critical attributes.

Maintaining a long-term perspective is vital for embracing change and uncertainty. While AI implementation may bring immediate challenges, the long-term benefits can be substantial. Leaders should keep the organization focused on the strategic vision and the transformative potential of AI, even when facing short-term setbacks. This forward-thinking approach helps maintain momentum and commitment to AI initiatives.

Building strong networks and partnerships can also help organizations navigate the uncertainties of the AI era.

Collaborating with industry peers, academic institutions, and technology providers can provide valuable insights, resources, and support. These partnerships can help organizations stay abreast of the latest developments in AI and share best practices for managing change.

Embracing change and uncertainty in the AI era involves cultivating a growth mindset, maintaining transparent communication, supporting employee development, encouraging experimentation, involving employees in the process, developing robust change management strategies, fostering resilience, maintaining a long-term perspective, and building strong networks. By adopting these practices, organizations can navigate the complexities of AI integration, drive innovation, and achieve sustainable success. Developing resilience and agility in the face of AI-driven disruptions is essential for organizations aiming to navigate the complexities and uncertainties brought by rapid technological advancements. Leaders must cultivate a culture that values adaptability and continuous learning, encouraging employees to view disruptions as opportunities for growth and innovation rather than threats. This involves fostering an environment where change is embraced and employees are empowered to respond proactively to new challenges.

Effective communication is crucial for building resilience and agility. Leaders should maintain transparent and open lines of communication about the potential impacts of AI, both positive and negative. Clearly articulating the strategic importance of AI and how it aligns with the organization's long-term goals helps build a shared understanding and commitment to navigating disruptions together. Regular updates on AI initiatives, including progress and setbacks, ensure that employees are informed and engaged.

Supporting employees through disruptions requires providing the necessary tools and resources for continuous development. Offering comprehensive training programs that focus on building relevant skills for the AI era, such as data literacy, technical proficiency, and problem-solving, equips employees to handle new tasks and challenges effectively. Encouraging a growth mindset, where employees see disruptions as learning opportunities, fosters a culture of resilience and adaptability.

Creating a supportive environment that encourages experimentation and innovation is key to developing agility. Organizations should promote a culture where taking calculated risks is encouraged, and failures are viewed as part of the learning process. Allowing room for trial and error enables teams to explore new ideas and refine their approaches based on real-world feedback. Celebrating both successes and lessons learned from failures reinforces the value of innovation and continuous improvement. Involving employees in the process of managing AI-driven disruptions helps build a sense of ownership and collaboration. Soliciting input and feedback from employees at all levels ensures that diverse perspectives are considered, leading to more robust and effective strategies. This participatory approach also helps identify potential issues early and fosters a collective commitment to overcoming challenges.

Developing robust change management strategies is essential for maintaining agility. This involves setting clear objectives, timelines, and metrics for AI initiatives and regularly reviewing progress to ensure alignment with strategic goals. Being flexible and ready to adjust plans based on new information or emerging challenges ensures that the organization remains responsive and adaptive. Leaders should provide guidance and support to teams as they navigate the complexities of AI integration, helping them stay focused and resilient.

Building strong networks and partnerships can enhance organizational resilience. Collaborating with industry peers, academic institutions, and technology providers offers valuable insights, resources, and support. These partnerships help organizations stay abreast of the latest developments in AI and share best practices for managing disruptions. Leveraging external expertise and resources can accelerate the organization's ability to adapt and innovate.

Maintaining a long-term perspective is vital for developing resilience and agility. While AI-driven disruptions may present immediate challenges, the long-term benefits can be substantial. Leaders should keep the organization focused on the strategic vision and the transformative potential of AI, even when facing short-term setbacks. This forward-thinking approach helps maintain momentum and commitment to AI initiatives, ensuring sustained progress and success.

Fostering a culture of continuous improvement involves encouraging employees to develop skills that enhance their adaptability and problem-solving abilities. Providing opportunities for professional development, coaching, and mentoring helps build a workforce that is capable of navigating disruptions with confidence and agility. Recognizing and rewarding resilience in the face of change reinforces its importance and motivates employees to develop these critical attributes. Developing resilience and agility in the face of AI-driven disruptions involves cultivating a growth mindset, maintaining transparent communication, supporting continuous development, encouraging experimentation, involving employees in the process, developing robust change management strategies, building strong networks, maintaining a long-term perspective, and fostering a culture of continuous improvement. By adopting these practices, organizations can navigate the complexities of AI integration, drive innovation, and achieve sustainable success in a rapidly evolving technological landscape.

Learning about systems thinking and AI is essential for understanding the complex, interconnected nature of modern technological environments. Systems thinking is an approach that views problems as parts of an overall system, rather than isolated components. This perspective is particularly valuable in AI, where the integration and interaction of various elements—data, algorithms, human users, and organizational processes—must be considered to achieve effective solutions. To begin with, systems thinking involves recognizing the interdependencies within a system. In the context of AI, this means understanding how data sources, machine learning models, user interfaces, and organizational goals interact and influence one another. By adopting a holistic view, individuals can better appreciate the broader impact of AI initiatives and anticipate potential ripple effects across different parts of the organization.

Developing a deep understanding of AI requires familiarity with its foundational concepts. This includes knowledge of data science, machine learning, neural networks, natural language processing, and other core technologies. Grasping these concepts helps individuals understand how AI systems are built and how they function, which is crucial for both development and effective implementation.

Practical experience is key to mastering systems thinking and AI. Engaging with real-world AI projects allows individuals to apply theoretical knowledge, see how various components interact in practice, and learn from the challenges and successes of implementation. This hands-on approach helps build a deeper understanding of both the technical and organizational aspects of AI. Continuous learning is essential in the rapidly evolving field of AI. Staying updated with the latest research, advancements, and best practices ensures that individuals remain proficient in cutting-edge technologies and methodologies. Participating in professional development opportunities, such as workshops, conferences, and online courses, supports ongoing education and skill enhancement.

Collaboration and knowledge sharing are integral to systems thinking and AI. Working with cross-functional teams that include data scientists, engineers, business analysts, and domain experts fosters a richer understanding of how AI can be applied to solve complex problems. Sharing insights and experiences through internal forums, discussion groups, and collaborative platforms enhances collective learning and innovation.

Ethical considerations are paramount in systems thinking and AI. Understanding the ethical implications of AI, such as bias, privacy, and accountability, is critical for responsible development and deployment. Adopting ethical guidelines and frameworks helps ensure that AI systems are designed and used in ways that align with organizational values and societal expectations.

Reflecting on feedback and outcomes is crucial for refining systems thinking and AI practices. Regularly evaluating the performance and impact of AI systems helps identify areas for improvement and ensures that initiatives remain aligned with strategic goals. Learning from both successes and failures informs future projects and contributes to continuous improvement.

Learning about systems thinking and AI involves understanding the interconnected nature of AI systems, mastering foundational concepts, gaining practical experience, committing to continuous learning, collaborating across functions, considering ethical implications, and reflecting on feedback and outcomes. By adopting this comprehensive approach, individuals and organizations can effectively leverage AI to drive innovation and achieve sustainable success.

Fostering a culture of continuous learning and improvement for AI is essential for organizations to remain competitive and innovative. This begins with leadership commitment to creating an environment that values education and growth. Leaders should model a mindset of lifelong learning, demonstrating their own engagement with AI advancements and encouraging employees to do the same.

A key element is providing comprehensive training programs that cater to different levels of AI expertise within the organization. Offering workshops, online courses, and certifications helps employees build and enhance their skills. These educational opportunities should cover fundamental AI concepts, practical applications, and emerging trends to ensure a well-rounded understanding. Encouraging hands-on experience is vital. Allowing employees to work on AI projects, participate in hackathons, and engage in experimentation fosters practical learning and innovation. This hands-on approach helps individuals apply theoretical knowledge to real-world scenarios, deepening their understanding and fostering creativity.

Creating a supportive environment where employees feel safe to take risks and learn from failures is crucial. Organizations should promote a culture that views mistakes as learning opportunities rather than setbacks. Celebrating both successes and the lessons learned from failures reinforces the importance of continuous improvement and resilience.

Promoting collaboration and knowledge sharing across the organization enhances learning. Establishing internal forums, discussion groups, and collaborative platforms enables employees to share insights, experiences, and best practices. This collective learning approach leverages the diverse expertise within the organization and drives innovation.

Ensuring access to the latest tools and resources is essential for continuous learning. Providing employees with up-to-date AI platforms, data sets, and development environments allows them to explore new technologies and methodologies. Staying current with industry advancements ensures that the organization remains at the forefront of AI innovation. Regularly evaluating and updating training programs to reflect new developments and organizational needs is important. This ensures that learning opportunities remain relevant and effective. Soliciting feedback from employees about their learning experiences helps identify areas for improvement and tailor programs to better meet their needs.

Recognizing and rewarding continuous learning efforts motivates employees to engage with educational opportunities. Highlighting achievements, such as completing courses or contributing to successful AI projects, reinforces the value of learning and encourages others to pursue similar goals.

Embedding a mindset of continuous improvement into the organizational culture involves setting clear expectations for ongoing development. Leaders should communicate the importance of staying current with AI advancements and integrating new knowledge into daily work practices. Encouraging employees to regularly review their skills and seek out learning opportunities supports this mindset. Fostering a culture of continuous learning and improvement for AI involves leadership commitment, comprehensive training programs, hands-on experience, a supportive environment, collaboration, access to resources, regular evaluation, recognition, and clear expectations. By creating an environment that values and supports ongoing education and growth, organizations can effectively leverage AI technologies, drive innovation, and achieve long-term success.

Part IV: Perspectives on AI and Leadership

Part IV: Perspectives on AI and Leadership delves into the diverse viewpoints surrounding the integration of AI in leadership roles. This section aims to provide a comprehensive understanding of how AI can influence, enhance, and potentially transform leadership functions. By examining different perspectives, we can better appreciate the multifaceted nature of AI's impact on leadership and the ethical considerations that accompany its rise.

Chapter 11 explores the enhancement perspective, where AI is seen as an additional assistance to current leadership functions. AI's capabilities in enhancing productivity and decision-making are highlighted through various case studies and examples of successful AI integration in leadership. This perspective underscores the potential benefits of AI as a supportive tool that complements and augments human leaders, enabling them to perform their roles more effectively.

Chapter 12 discusses the replacement perspective, which considers AI's potential to replace both followers and leaders. This chapter explores the ethical considerations and potential impacts of AI-driven leadership, presenting scenarios where AI takes on more autonomous leadership roles. The implications of such a shift are examined, raising important questions about the nature of leadership and the evolving dynamics between humans and AI in the workplace.

Chapter 13 presents the skeptical perspective, evaluating the limitations of AI in leadership. This chapter emphasizes the importance of human emotional intelligence and complex decision-making skills that AI currently lacks. A critical analysis of AI's current and future capabilities is provided, arguing that while AI can support leadership functions, it cannot fully replicate the nuanced and empathetic aspects of human leadership.

The conclusion of Part IV provides a summary of the book, recapping the key insights and recommendations discussed throughout. It reflects on the future of leadership in the AI era, emphasizing the need for leaders to embrace AI while remaining mindful of its limitations and ethical implications. The conclusion serves as a call to action for leaders to shape the impact of AI proactively, ensuring that its integration into leadership roles is guided by a commitment to enhancing human potential and organizational success.

Chapter 11: Enhancement Perspective

AI as an additional assistance to current leadership functions represents a transformative shift in how leaders can enhance their effectiveness and efficiency. AI technologies provide tools that augment traditional leadership roles by improving decision-making, increasing productivity, and offering new insights through advanced data analytics. Leaders can leverage AI to handle routine and administrative tasks, allowing them to focus more on strategic planning, innovation, and interpersonal aspects of their roles.

One of the primary benefits of AI is its ability to process and analyze vast amounts of data quickly and accurately. This capability enables leaders to make more informed decisions based on real-time data and predictive analytics. For example, AI can analyze market trends, customer feedback, and internal performance metrics to provide actionable insights that guide strategic initiatives. By relying on data-driven insights, leaders can minimize the risk of bias and make more objective decisions.

AI also enhances productivity by automating repetitive and time-consuming tasks. Administrative functions such as scheduling meetings, managing emails, and generating reports can be efficiently handled by AI-powered tools. This automation frees up leaders' time, allowing them to focus on high-impact activities that require human judgment and creativity. Additionally, AI can streamline workflows and improve operational efficiency by identifying bottlenecks and suggesting process improvements. AI can assist leaders in talent management and development. AI-driven platforms can analyze employee performance data to identify skill gaps, recommend personalized training programs, and even predict future staffing needs. This enables leaders to make proactive decisions about talent acquisition and development, ensuring that their teams are equipped with the necessary skills to meet organizational goals.

AI can enhance communication and collaboration within teams. AI-powered virtual assistants and chatbots can facilitate real-time communication and information sharing, reducing delays and improving responsiveness. These tools can also help leaders stay connected with their teams, providing updates, answering questions, and gathering feedback efficiently.

Case studies and examples of successful AI integration in leadership functions demonstrate the tangible benefits of these technologies. For instance, companies like IBM and General Electric have implemented AI-driven analytics to optimize decision-making and improve operational efficiency. AI-powered HR platforms such as Workday and SAP SuccessFactors are used to enhance talent management processes. These examples highlight how AI can be seamlessly integrated into leadership functions to drive better outcomes.

While AI offers numerous advantages, it is important for leaders to approach its integration thoughtfully. AI should be seen as a tool that complements human capabilities rather than replaces them. The interpersonal skills, empathy, and emotional intelligence that leaders bring to their roles are irreplaceable by machines. Therefore, successful AI integration involves finding the right balance between leveraging AI for efficiency and retaining the human touch that is essential for effective leadership.

AI as an additional assistance to current leadership functions provides significant opportunities to enhance decision-making, productivity, and overall effectiveness. By automating routine tasks, offering data-driven insights, and improving communication, AI allows leaders to focus on strategic and high-impact activities. Real-world examples underscore the potential of AI to transform leadership functions, but it is crucial to maintain a balance that preserves the human elements of leadership. Embracing AI as a supportive tool can empower leaders to drive innovation and achieve organizational success in the AI era.

Enhancing productivity and decision-making through AI integration is transforming leadership functions. AI technologies enable leaders to process vast amounts of data quickly and accurately, providing insights that inform strategic decisions. By leveraging predictive analytics, leaders can anticipate market trends, customer behaviors, and internal performance metrics, leading to more informed and objective decision-making. This minimizes the risk of bias and enhances the quality of decisions made.

AI serves as a powerful tool to enhance current leadership functions by supporting decision-making processes, providing data-driven insights, and delivering real-time analytics. This additional assistance allows leaders to make more informed and strategic decisions, improving overall organizational effectiveness and responsiveness. AI also supports leaders in decision-making processes by automating the analysis of large datasets, identifying patterns, and predicting future trends. These capabilities enable leaders to base their decisions on comprehensive and accurate information rather than intuition or limited data. For instance, AI can analyze market trends, customer behavior, and competitive actions to offer strategic recommendations that align with organizational goals. By processing this information quickly, AI helps leaders respond to changes in the environment with agility and precision.

One of AI's most significant roles is in providing data-driven insights and real-time analytics. AI systems can continuously collect and analyze data from various sources, offering leaders up-to-date information that is crucial for timely decision-making. For example, in a retail setting, AI can monitor sales data, inventory levels, and customer feedback in real-time, allowing leaders to adjust marketing strategies, stock levels, and customer service approaches instantaneously. This capability ensures that leaders have access to the latest information, reducing the risk of making decisions based on outdated or incomplete data.

There are numerous examples of AI tools that enhance leadership effectiveness. Predictive analytics platforms such as IBM Watson provide leaders with insights into future trends and potential outcomes based on historical data. These platforms help leaders anticipate challenges and opportunities, enabling proactive strategy adjustments. Another example is the use of AI-powered customer relationship management (CRM) systems like Salesforce Einstein, which analyze customer interactions and preferences to offer personalized recommendations for engagement and sales strategies. This enhances customer satisfaction and loyalty, driving business growth. Additionally, AI-driven project management tools like Asana and Trello use machine learning algorithms to optimize task assignments, track project progress, and predict potential bottlenecks. These tools provide leaders with a clear overview of project status and resource allocation, improving efficiency and ensuring timely project completion. Similarly, AI in human resources management, through platforms like Workday, assists leaders in identifying talent gaps, predicting employee turnover, and developing targeted training programs. This enhances workforce planning and development, ensuring that the organization remains agile and competitive.

Enhancing productivity and decision-making through AI integration has a profound impact on operational efficiency and strategic planning. By automating routine tasks, optimizing processes, and providing data-driven insights, AI significantly enhances the productivity of organizations and enables leaders to make more informed, strategic decisions.

The impact of AI on improving operational efficiency is evident in its ability to automate repetitive and time-consuming tasks. In manufacturing, for example, AI-driven robotics and automation systems streamline production lines, reducing the need for manual labor and minimizing human error. This leads to higher output and improved product quality. Similarly, in customer service, AI-powered chatbots handle routine inquiries, freeing up human agents to focus on more complex issues. This not only increases the efficiency of customer service operations but also enhances customer satisfaction by providing faster responses.

New case studies demonstrating AI-driven productivity gains highlight the tangible benefits of AI integration. For instance, General Electric (GE) implemented AI in its maintenance operations, utilizing predictive analytics to forecast equipment failures before they occur. This proactive approach reduced unplanned downtime by 20%, leading to significant cost savings and increased productivity. Another example is Procter & Gamble (P&G), which used AI to optimize its supply chain. By analyzing data from various sources, including weather patterns, consumer behavior, and transportation logistics, P&G improved its demand forecasting accuracy, reduced excess inventory, and enhanced overall supply chain efficiency. This resulted in a more responsive and cost-effective operation.

AI also aids in strategic decision-making and planning by providing leaders with comprehensive and actionable insights. Through advanced analytics, AI can process vast amounts of data from multiple sources to identify trends, correlations, and potential risks. For example, in the financial sector, AI algorithms analyze market data to predict stock price movements, helping portfolio managers make better investment decisions. Similarly, in healthcare, AI analyzes patient data to identify disease patterns and recommend personalized treatment plans, enabling healthcare providers to improve patient outcomes and optimize resource allocation.

Strategic planning benefits from AI's ability to simulate various scenarios and predict outcomes. AI tools like scenario analysis and simulation modeling allow leaders to test different strategies and evaluate their potential impact before implementation. This capability helps organizations anticipate challenges and make more resilient plans. For example, in urban planning, AI models can simulate the impact of new infrastructure projects on traffic patterns, environmental sustainability, and economic growth, enabling planners to make data-informed decisions that balance multiple objectives.

AI enhances decision-making by reducing cognitive biases that often influence human judgment. By relying on objective data and sophisticated algorithms, AI provides a more balanced perspective, allowing leaders to make decisions based on evidence rather than intuition or incomplete information. This leads to more accurate and effective strategies that align with organizational goals and market demands. Personalized leadership development through AI offers a transformative approach to identifying individual strengths and weaknesses, tailoring coaching and development programs, and providing personalized feedback for continuous improvement.

AI plays a crucial role in identifying individual strengths and weaknesses. By analyzing a variety of data points, including performance metrics, behavioral assessments, and peer feedback, AI can generate comprehensive profiles of leaders. These profiles highlight areas where individuals excel and where they may need further development. For example, AI-driven platforms like IBM Watson Talent can assess leadership competencies by analyzing data from 360-degree feedback surveys and performance reviews. This granular analysis provides a detailed understanding of a leader's capabilities, enabling targeted development efforts.

Once strengths and weaknesses are identified, AI can tailor coaching and development programs to address specific needs. Personalized learning paths can be created, incorporating various resources such as e-learning modules, virtual coaching sessions, and experiential learning opportunities. AI can recommend specific training materials, workshops, or mentorship programs that align with the individual's development goals. For instance, platforms like Coursera for Business use AI to suggest courses based on an individual's job role, career aspirations, and skill gaps. This tailored approach ensures that leaders receive relevant and impactful development experiences.

The benefits of personalized feedback and continuous improvement through AI are substantial. AI systems can provide real-time feedback, enabling leaders to adjust their behaviors and strategies promptly. For example, AI-powered tools like BetterUp use data from leadership assessments and interactions to offer instant feedback and actionable insights. This continuous feedback loop helps leaders refine their skills and adapt to new challenges more effectively.

Personalized feedback is also more precise and relevant, as it is based on comprehensive data analysis rather than generic assessment criteria. This precision increases the likelihood that leaders will engage with and act on the feedback, leading to more significant improvements in performance. Additionally, AI can track progress over time, highlighting improvements and remaining areas for development. This ongoing monitoring supports a culture of continuous improvement, where leaders are encouraged to keep developing their skills and adapting to changing organizational needs.

AI-driven personalized leadership development fosters greater engagement and motivation among leaders. When development programs are tailored to individual needs and preferences, leaders are more likely to find them meaningful and relevant. This personalized approach demonstrates that the organization values and invests in their growth, which can enhance job satisfaction and retention.

Leveraging AI for sentiment analysis and team management significantly enhances emotional intelligence and team dynamics within an organization. AI technologies can analyze vast amounts of communication data, such as emails, chat messages, and meeting transcripts, to gauge the emotional tone and sentiment of team interactions. This provides leaders with valuable insights into the overall mood and morale of their teams, enabling proactive management of any issues that arise.

Understanding and managing emotions with AI insights involves using data-driven approaches to assess and respond to the emotional states of team members. AI tools like sentiment analysis algorithms can detect signs of stress, frustration, or disengagement in real-time. For example, an AI system might analyze a series of team messages and identify a pattern of negative sentiment, indicating potential dissatisfaction or conflict. Armed with this information, leaders can intervene early, addressing concerns before they escalate and providing support where needed.

AI insights can also help leaders tailor their communication and management styles to better align with the emotional needs of their team members. By understanding how different individuals respond to various situations, leaders can adopt more empathetic and effective approaches. For instance, if AI analysis reveals that a team member responds positively to frequent feedback and recognition, a leader can ensure these elements are incorporated into their interactions with that individual.

Fostering collaboration and cohesion within teams through AI is another critical application. AI can identify collaboration patterns and suggest ways to enhance teamwork. For instance, AI tools can track how often team members communicate and collaborate on projects, identifying both strong partnerships and potential silos. This information enables leaders to facilitate better connections among team members, encouraging more inclusive and cooperative work environments.

AI-driven platforms can also recommend team-building activities and strategies based on the specific dynamics and needs of the team. For example, if AI analysis indicates that a team struggles with trust or communication, a leader might organize workshops or social activities designed to strengthen these areas. Additionally, AI can provide personalized development plans that include training on emotional intelligence and collaboration skills, further enhancing team dynamics. AI can also enhance remote team management by providing insights into the virtual interactions of team members. As remote work becomes more common, maintaining strong team dynamics can be challenging. AI tools can monitor virtual communication channels and offer leaders a clear picture of how well the team is functioning, even from a distance. This ensures that leaders can maintain high levels of engagement and cohesion, regardless of physical location.

AI can facilitate more effective conflict resolution. By analyzing past interactions and outcomes, AI can help leaders understand the root causes of conflicts and identify patterns that may lead to future disputes. This proactive approach allows leaders to address underlying issues before they become major problems, fostering a more harmonious and productive team environment. AI serves as a powerful catalyst for creative problem-solving and innovation. By processing and analyzing vast amounts of data, AI can uncover patterns and insights that may not be immediately apparent to humans. This ability enables organizations to identify new opportunities for innovation and develop creative solutions to complex problems. For instance, AI-driven platforms can generate ideas for new products or services by analyzing consumer preferences, market trends, and historical data. These insights can lead to the development of innovative offerings that meet emerging customer needs and drive business growth.

Identifying emerging trends and opportunities with AI involves leveraging predictive analytics and machine learning algorithms to forecast future developments. AI systems can analyze data from various sources, including social media, market reports, and industry publications, to detect early signs of shifts in consumer behavior, technological advancements, and competitive dynamics. By staying ahead of these trends, organizations can proactively adjust their strategies and capitalize on new opportunities. For example, a retail company might use AI to predict upcoming fashion trends and adjust its inventory and marketing strategies, accordingly, ensuring it remains relevant and competitive.

Implementing innovative strategies for competitive advantage requires a thoughtful integration of AI capabilities into business processes. AI can enhance product development cycles, streamline operations, and improve customer experiences, all of which contribute to a competitive edge. For example, AI-powered recommendation engines can personalize customer interactions, increasing engagement and loyalty. In manufacturing, AI can optimize supply chains and production processes, reducing costs and improving efficiency. By continuously exploring and adopting AI-driven innovations, organizations can maintain their competitive advantage and drive sustained growth.

The importance of maintaining the human touch in leadership cannot be overstated. While AI can provide valuable insights and automate routine tasks, human qualities such as empathy, creativity, and ethical judgment remain crucial for effective leadership. Leaders must ensure that AI complements rather than replaces these human attributes. By combining the analytical power of AI with the emotional intelligence of human leaders, organizations can achieve a balanced approach that leverages the strengths of both.

Ethical considerations and the limitations of AI are essential factors to address in this integration. AI systems can inadvertently perpetuate biases present in their training data, leading to unfair or discriminatory outcomes. Additionally, AI lacks the moral reasoning and contextual understanding that humans possess. Leaders must establish robust ethical guidelines and governance frameworks to ensure AI is used responsibly. This includes regular audits of AI systems for bias, transparency in AI decision-making processes, and a commitment to ethical principles in AI deployment.

Strategies for integrating AI without losing human values involve fostering a collaborative environment where AI and human capabilities are seen as complementary. This can be achieved by:

- Promoting a culture of continuous learning: Encourage employees to develop their skills and understanding of AI technologies, ensuring they can work effectively alongside AI systems.

- Involving employees in AI implementation: Seek input from employees on how AI can be integrated into their workflows and address any concerns they may have about its impact.
- Emphasizing ethical AI use: Implement training programs on ethical AI practices and ensure that ethical considerations are embedded in AI development and deployment processes.

- Encouraging human-AI collaboration: Design workflows that leverage AI for data analysis and routine tasks while allowing humans to focus on strategic, creative, and interpersonal aspects of their roles.

Fostering innovation through AI and balancing human and AI capabilities are critical for modern leadership. AI can drive creative problem-solving, identify emerging trends, and implement innovative strategies that provide a competitive advantage. However, maintaining the human touch, addressing ethical considerations, and integrating AI responsibly are essential to ensuring that AI serves as an enhancement rather than a replacement for human leadership. By adopting these approaches, organizations can harness the full potential of AI while preserving the values and qualities that make effective leadership possible.

The future outlook for AI in leadership is promising, with significant advancements expected to continue shaping how leaders operate and make decisions. Predictions for the continued evolution of AI in leadership indicate that AI will become even more integrated into everyday business processes, providing leaders with more sophisticated tools to enhance their effectiveness. AI technologies will increasingly automate routine tasks, allowing leaders to focus on strategic, creative, and interpersonal aspects of their roles. As AI algorithms become more advanced, they will provide deeper insights and more accurate predictions, enabling leaders to make better-informed decisions.

Emerging AI technologies that will further enhance leadership capabilities include advancements in natural language processing (NLP), emotional AI, and augmented analytics. NLP advancements will improve the way leaders interact with AI systems, making communication more intuitive and enabling more effective use of AI-driven insights. Emotional AI will enhance leaders' ability to understand and respond to team members' emotions, improving team dynamics and employee engagement. Augmented analytics will combine AI and human intelligence to provide more actionable insights, supporting data-driven decision-making and strategic planning.

Long-term benefits of AI augmentation in leadership include increased efficiency, improved decision-making, and enhanced innovation. AI will enable leaders to manage operations more effectively, optimize resource allocation, and identify new opportunities for growth. By leveraging AI's predictive capabilities, leaders can anticipate market trends and potential disruptions, allowing for proactive rather than reactive strategies. This will result in more resilient and adaptable organizations, capable of navigating complex and dynamic environments.

There are also potential challenges associated with AI augmentation in leadership. One significant challenge is the risk of over-reliance on AI, which could lead to a loss of critical thinking and human judgment. Leaders must ensure that AI serves as a complement to, rather than a replacement for, human decision-making. Ethical considerations will also remain a crucial concern, as AI systems must be designed and used in ways that are fair, transparent, and accountable. Addressing biases in AI algorithms, ensuring data privacy, and maintaining ethical standards will be essential to prevent negative outcomes.

Another potential challenge is the impact on the workforce. As AI automates more tasks, there may be concerns about job displacement and the need for reskilling and upskilling employees. Organizations must invest in continuous learning and development programs to help their workforce adapt to new roles that require collaboration with AI technologies. Fostering a culture of innovation and adaptability will be key to managing these transitions and ensuring that employees remain engaged and productive.

The future outlook for AI in leadership is marked by significant opportunities for enhancing leadership capabilities and driving organizational success. Emerging AI technologies will provide leaders with powerful tools to improve decision-making, foster innovation, and optimize operations. However, addressing the potential challenges of AI augmentation, such as ethical considerations, workforce impacts, and the risk of over-reliance on technology, will be crucial. By balancing the strengths of AI with the unique qualities of human leadership, organizations can harness the full potential of AI while maintaining the values and principles that underpin effective leadership.

Chapter 12: Replacement Perspective

The replacement perspective on AI in leadership examines the transformative potential of artificial intelligence not just to augment human capabilities, but to potentially replace certain roles traditionally held by humans. This perspective explores how advanced AI systems could assume tasks and responsibilities of both followers and leaders, reshaping organizational dynamics and operational structures.

The potential for AI to replace followers is evident in the automation of routine and repetitive tasks. Many roles that involve predictable, rules-based activities are increasingly being managed by AI systems. For example, administrative tasks, data entry, customer service interactions, and even some aspects of project management can be efficiently handled by AI, reducing the need for human involvement in these areas. This shift allows organizations to optimize efficiency and cost-effectiveness, but also raises significant questions about job displacement and the future of the workforce.

More intriguingly, AI's potential to replace leaders is becoming a topic of serious consideration. AI systems equipped with advanced decision-making capabilities and real-time data processing can theoretically perform leadership functions such as strategic planning, resource allocation, and performance evaluation. AI-driven leaders could analyze vast amounts of information, identify trends, and make decisions without the biases that often affect human judgment. Scenarios where AI assumes leadership roles might include managing operational workflows, optimizing logistics, or even leading teams in data-driven environments where quick, evidence-based decisions are crucial.

The replacement of human leaders with AI presents both ethical and practical considerations. Ethically, the delegation of leadership responsibilities to AI systems raises questions about accountability, transparency, and fairness. Who is responsible when an AI makes a decision that leads to unintended consequences? How can we ensure that AI-driven decisions are fair and unbiased, given that AI systems can inherit and even amplify existing biases in their training data? Additionally, there are concerns about the loss of the human touch in leadership – qualities such as empathy, emotional intelligence, and ethical reasoning that AI currently cannot replicate.

Practically, implementing AI-driven leadership involves significant challenges. Developing AI systems that are reliable, secure, and capable of handling complex leadership tasks is technically demanding. Organizations must also manage the transition to AI-driven leadership carefully to mitigate resistance from employees and stakeholders who may fear job loss or feel uncomfortable with AI oversight. Furthermore, regulatory and legal frameworks must evolve to address the unique challenges posed by AI in leadership roles, ensuring that AI is used responsibly and ethically.

AI has the transformative potential to replace followers in organizations by automating routine and repetitive tasks. This automation not only enhances efficiency and accuracy but also allows human workers to focus on more complex and creative activities that AI cannot handle. The growing sophistication of AI technologies makes it feasible to delegate a wide range of tasks to machines, fundamentally changing the landscape of employment and job roles.

One of the primary ways AI replaces followers is through the automation of routine and repetitive tasks. These tasks include data entry, scheduling, customer service interactions, and simple decision-making processes that follow clear, predefined rules. AI systems, such as robotic process automation (RPA) and chatbots, can perform these tasks more quickly and accurately than humans, reducing costs and increasing productivity. For example, RPA can streamline administrative processes by handling invoice processing, payroll management, and employee onboarding, while AI-powered chatbots can manage customer inquiries and provide instant support, minimizing the need for human intervention.

Examples of jobs and roles highly susceptible to AI replacement include those in sectors like customer service, manufacturing, and logistics. In customer service, AI chatbots and virtual assistants can handle a large volume of routine inquiries, freeing human agents to deal with more complex issues. In manufacturing, robots equipped with AI can perform assembly line tasks, quality control, and even predictive maintenance, reducing the need for manual labor. In logistics, AI systems can optimize routing, manage inventory, and track shipments in real-time, significantly reducing the need for human oversight. Data entry clerks, telemarketers, and basic accounting roles are also at high risk of being automated as AI technologies continue to advance.

The impact on employment and job displacement is a significant concern as AI increasingly replaces these roles. While AI can enhance productivity and create new opportunities, it also poses a risk of widespread job displacement, particularly for workers in low-skill positions. This displacement can lead to economic inequality and social unrest if not managed properly. The transition to an AI-driven workforce requires thoughtful strategies to mitigate these negative impacts.

Strategies for workforce transition and reskilling are essential to address the challenges posed by AI replacement. Organizations must invest in reskilling and upskilling programs to help employees transition to new roles that leverage human creativity, emotional intelligence, and complex problem-solving skills. This involves identifying the skills that will be in demand in the AI era and providing training and development opportunities to acquire those skills. For instance, programs focused on digital literacy, advanced analytics, critical thinking, and interpersonal communication can prepare workers for the evolving job market.

In addition to training programs, fostering a culture of continuous learning within organizations is crucial. Encouraging employees to embrace lifelong learning and providing them with the resources to do so can help them stay adaptable and competitive. Partnerships between businesses, educational institutions, and government agencies can facilitate this process, ensuring that workers have access to the necessary training and support.

Creating new job roles that complement AI technologies can help mitigate job displacement. As AI takes over routine tasks, there will be a growing need for roles that involve overseeing and maintaining AI systems, interpreting AI-generated insights, and applying these insights to strategic decision-making. By developing these complementary roles, organizations can ensure that human workers remain an integral part of the workforce.

AI's potential to replace leaders lies primarily in its autonomous decision-making capabilities. Advanced AI systems, equipped with machine learning and predictive analytics, can process vast amounts of data, recognize patterns, and make informed decisions faster than human leaders. These capabilities enable AI to analyze complex situations, evaluate potential outcomes, and recommend optimal courses of action. As AI technologies continue to evolve, the prospect of AI-driven leadership becomes more feasible, raising questions about the future of human leadership roles.

Scenarios where AI could assume leadership roles are varied and increasingly plausible. In strategic planning, AI could analyze market trends, competitor actions, and internal performance metrics to develop comprehensive business strategies. In project management, AI can allocate resources, track progress, and adjust timelines based on real-time data, ensuring projects stay on schedule and within budget. In financial management, AI systems can forecast revenues, manage investments, and optimize budgets by analyzing financial data and market conditions. Additionally, in customer relationship management, AI can personalize customer interactions, predict customer needs, and manage customer service teams, enhancing overall customer satisfaction.

The benefits of AI-driven leadership are numerous. AI systems can process and analyze data at a scale and speed beyond human capability, leading to more informed and objective decisions. This data-driven approach reduces the risk of biases that often affect human judgment, resulting in fairer and more consistent decision-making. AI's ability to operate continuously without fatigue or emotional influence ensures high efficiency and reliability in leadership tasks. Moreover, AI can provide real-time insights and predictive analytics, enabling proactive management and strategic planning. By handling routine and data-intensive tasks, AI allows human leaders to focus on more strategic and creative activities, enhancing overall organizational performance.

AI-driven leadership also has its limitations. One significant limitation is the lack of emotional intelligence. AI cannot understand or manage emotions, which are crucial for effective leadership. Building trust, fostering teamwork, and inspiring employees require empathy, compassion, and interpersonal skills that AI currently lacks. Additionally, AI systems are only as good as the data they are trained on, and any biases or inaccuracies in the data can lead to flawed decisions. The ethical implications of AI decision-making, such as accountability and transparency, also pose challenges. Determining who is responsible for AI-driven decisions, especially when they lead to negative outcomes, is complex and requires clear governance frameworks.

Human qualities that AI cannot replicate include empathy, intuition, creativity, and ethical reasoning. Empathy enables leaders to connect with their team members, understand their concerns, and provide support. This emotional connection builds trust and loyalty, essential for a cohesive and motivated workforce. Intuition allows leaders to make decisions based on experience and gut feelings, which can be particularly valuable in ambiguous or rapidly changing situations. Creativity drives innovation and problem-solving, enabling leaders to develop unique solutions and strategies. Ethical reasoning involves considering the broader impact of decisions on stakeholders and society, ensuring that actions align with moral and ethical standards. While AI can assist with data-driven insights, these human qualities are irreplaceable in effective leadership.

The integration of AI into leadership roles brings forth several ethical considerations and potential impacts that must be carefully managed to ensure responsible and fair use of these technologies. Key issues include accountability and transparency in AI decision-making, bias and fairness, privacy and data security, and the long-term societal implications of AI replacing human roles.

Accountability and transparency in AI decision-making are critical ethical concerns. When AI systems are used to make decisions, particularly those that affect people's lives and livelihoods, it is essential to establish clear lines of accountability. If an AI system makes a harmful decision, it can be challenging to determine who is responsible—the developers, the users, or the AI itself. To address this, organizations must implement robust governance frameworks that outline the responsibilities and oversight mechanisms for AI decision-making. Transparency is also crucial; stakeholders need to understand how AI systems reach their decisions. This involves making the decision-making processes of AI systems interpretable and explainable, ensuring that users can trust and verify the outcomes.

Bias and fairness in AI-driven leadership are significant concerns because AI systems can perpetuate or even exacerbate existing biases in the data they are trained on. This can lead to unfair and discriminatory outcomes, particularly in hiring, promotions, and resource allocation. Ensuring fairness requires rigorous testing and validation of AI systems to identify and mitigate biases. It also involves using diverse and representative datasets to train AI models and regularly updating these datasets to reflect changing societal norms and values. Organizations must prioritize fairness in AI development and deployment, implementing checks and balances to prevent biased decision-making.

Privacy and data security concerns are paramount when using AI in leadership roles. AI systems often require large amounts of personal data to function effectively, raising issues around data privacy and security. Organizations must comply with data protection regulations, such as the General Data Protection Regulation (GDPR) and the California Consumer Privacy Act (CCPA), to safeguard personal information. This includes implementing strong encryption, secure data storage, and access controls to protect against data breaches and unauthorized access. Additionally, organizations must be transparent with individuals about how their data is used and provide mechanisms for them to control their personal information.

Long-term societal implications of AI replacing human roles include potential impacts on employment, economic inequality, and social cohesion. As AI systems become more capable, they could displace many jobs, leading to significant shifts in the labor market. While AI can create new opportunities and roles, there is a risk that these benefits will not be evenly distributed, exacerbating economic disparities. To address this, policymakers and organizations must invest in education and training programs to reskill and upskill workers, ensuring they can transition to new roles that complement AI technologies. Additionally, social safety nets and support systems may need to be strengthened to help individuals and communities adapt to these changes.

Moreover, the widespread adoption of AI in leadership could impact social cohesion by altering how people interact with organizations and each other. As AI systems take on more decision-making roles, there may be a loss of human connection and empathy in organizational interactions. It is crucial to maintain a balance between AI and human involvement, ensuring that the human touch is preserved in areas where it is most needed, such as in team management, customer service, and community engagement.

Chapter 13: Skeptical Perspective

Evaluating the limitations of AI in leadership reveals several critical aspects that underscore the continued importance of human involvement in guiding organizations. One of the primary limitations of AI in leadership is its inability to exhibit emotional intelligence. Leadership often involves understanding and managing emotions, both one's own and those of team members. AI lacks the capacity for empathy, making it difficult to navigate complex interpersonal dynamics and build trust and rapport with employees. This emotional disconnect can lead to a less cohesive and motivated workforce, as AI cannot provide the personal touch that human leaders bring.

AI also struggles with creative and intuitive decision-making. While AI excels at analyzing data and identifying patterns, it lacks the innate human ability to think creatively and generate innovative solutions. Leadership frequently requires out-of-the-box thinking and the ability to adapt to unforeseen challenges with novel approaches. Human leaders draw on their experiences, insights, and intuition to make decisions that go beyond data-driven analysis. This creativity and adaptability are crucial for driving innovation and responding effectively to dynamic market conditions.

Another limitation of AI in leadership is its dependency on data quality and availability. AI systems require vast amounts of high-quality data to function effectively. In situations where data is scarce, incomplete, or biased, AI's decision-making capabilities can be significantly compromised. Human leaders, on the other hand, can often make informed decisions even with limited or imperfect information, using their judgment and expertise to fill in the gaps.

Ethical considerations present further challenges for AI leadership. AI systems can inadvertently perpetuate biases present in the data they are trained on, leading to unfair and discriminatory outcomes. Addressing these biases requires continuous monitoring and intervention by human overseers. Moreover, ethical dilemmas often involve complex trade-offs that require moral reasoning and a deep understanding of societal values, which AI lacks. Human leaders are better equipped to navigate these ethical challenges, ensuring that decisions align with organizational values and ethical standards.

The issue of accountability is also significant when considering AI in leadership roles. Determining responsibility for decisions made by AI systems can be complex, especially when these decisions have far-reaching consequences. Clear accountability structures are essential to ensure that AI operates within defined ethical and legal boundaries. Human leaders are inherently accountable for their actions and decisions, providing a clear line of responsibility that is essential for maintaining trust and integrity within an organization.

AI's limitations in understanding context and nuance further highlight its inadequacy in fully replacing human leaders. Leadership decisions often require a deep understanding of contextual factors and subtle nuances that AI may not grasp. This includes cultural considerations, organizational history, and the unique dynamics of specific teams or individuals. Human leaders can interpret and respond to these subtleties in ways that AI cannot, ensuring more tailored and effective leadership.

The potential impact on organizational culture and employee morale cannot be overlooked. AI-driven leadership may lead to a more transactional and impersonal work environment, where decisions are perceived as detached from the human experience. Human leaders play a crucial role in fostering a positive organizational culture, inspiring employees, and creating a sense of purpose and belonging. The absence of these human elements can negatively affect employee engagement and overall organizational health.

While AI offers valuable tools for enhancing leadership capabilities, it has significant limitations that prevent it from fully replacing human leaders. Emotional intelligence, creativity, ethical reasoning, accountability, contextual understanding, and the ability to foster a positive organizational culture are all areas where human leaders excel. These limitations underscore the need for a balanced approach, where AI supports and augments human leadership rather than attempting to replace it. By leveraging the strengths of both AI and human leaders, organizations can navigate the complexities of modern leadership and achieve sustainable success.

The importance of human emotional intelligence and complex decision-making in leadership cannot be overstated, especially in an era increasingly influenced by AI. Emotional intelligence, the ability to understand and manage one's own emotions and those of others, is a cornerstone of effective leadership. It enables leaders to build strong relationships, foster teamwork, and create a positive organizational culture. Human leaders use emotional intelligence to navigate interpersonal dynamics, resolve conflicts, and motivate employees. This emotional connection builds trust and loyalty, crucial for maintaining a cohesive and motivated workforce. Complex decision-making often involves nuanced judgment and consideration of multiple factors that AI might not fully comprehend. Human leaders draw on their experience, intuition, and understanding of context to make decisions that are not solely data-driven. They can interpret subtle cues, weigh ethical considerations, and consider long-term implications in ways that AI currently cannot. This ability to integrate various perspectives and foresee the broader impact of decisions is essential for strategic planning and organizational success.

Human leaders can adapt to changing circumstances with a level of flexibility and creativity that AI lacks. They can think outside the box, generate innovative solutions, and pivot strategies in response to unforeseen challenges. This adaptability is critical in today's fast-paced business environment, where the ability to quickly respond to new information and evolving market conditions can determine success or failure.

The personal touch that human leaders bring to their roles also plays a significant role in employee engagement and morale. Leaders who exhibit empathy, compassion, and understanding can create an inclusive and supportive work environment. They recognize and value the unique contributions of each team member, fostering a sense of belonging and purpose. This emotional support can enhance job satisfaction, reduce turnover, and improve overall organizational performance.

Ethical decision-making is another area where human leaders excel. They can navigate complex moral dilemmas, consider the impact of their decisions on various stakeholders, and align their actions with the organization's values. While AI can assist with data analysis and suggest potential outcomes, it lacks the moral reasoning and ethical judgment that human leaders possess. Ensuring decisions are fair, just, and ethically sound is a fundamental aspect of leadership that requires a human touch.

Human emotional intelligence and complex decision-making are vital components of effective leadership. These qualities enable leaders to build strong relationships, navigate complex situations, adapt to change, and make ethical decisions. While AI can enhance certain aspects of leadership by providing data-driven insights, it cannot replace the uniquely human abilities that are essential for leading organizations successfully. Therefore, a balanced approach that leverages the strengths of both AI and human leaders is crucial for achieving sustainable success in the modern business landscape.

A critical analysis of AI's current capabilities reveals both its significant strengths and notable limitations. AI excels in processing vast amounts of data quickly and accurately, making it invaluable for tasks that involve pattern recognition, data analysis, and predictive modeling. These capabilities allow AI to outperform humans in areas requiring high-speed computations and large-scale data management, such as financial forecasting, supply chain optimization, and customer behavior analysis. However, AI's reliance on data is also a major limitation. The effectiveness of AI systems is contingent on the quality and quantity of the data they are trained on. Incomplete, biased, or inaccurate data can lead to flawed outcomes and reinforce existing biases. Unlike humans, AI cannot draw on experience or intuition to fill in gaps where data is lacking or unclear. This dependency on data quality restricts AI's ability to function effectively in situations where data is sparse or unreliable.

AI also struggles with tasks that require emotional intelligence and nuanced understanding. While AI can process and analyze text and speech for sentiment, it lacks the ability to truly understand and empathize with human emotions. This deficiency limits AI's effectiveness in roles that involve complex human interactions, such as counseling, negotiation, and leadership. The inability to genuinely connect with people on an emotional level is a fundamental barrier to AI fully replicating human-centric roles.

Another limitation is AI's lack of creativity and innovation. AI can generate solutions based on existing patterns and data but lacks the ability to think outside the box or come up with novel ideas that break from historical data. This restricts AI's usefulness in fields that require creative problem-solving and innovation, such as strategic planning and artistic endeavors.

Ethical and moral reasoning is another area where AI falls short. AI can be programmed with ethical guidelines, but it lacks the inherent understanding of complex moral dilemmas that humans possess. This limitation becomes particularly significant in areas like law enforcement, healthcare, and autonomous driving, where decisions can have profound ethical implications. The absence of genuine moral reasoning in AI systems necessitates human oversight to ensure ethical standards are upheld.

Accountability in AI decision-making presents another challenge. Determining responsibility for the outcomes of AI-driven decisions can be complex, especially when these decisions lead to unintended consequences. Clear frameworks for accountability are essential, but they are difficult to establish given AI's autonomous nature and the potential for human operators to distance themselves from responsibility.

AI's current capabilities also raise concerns about job displacement and economic inequality. While AI can enhance productivity and efficiency, it can also automate tasks traditionally performed by humans, leading to job losses and economic disruption. Addressing these socio-economic impacts requires thoughtful strategies, such as reskilling and upskilling programs, to ensure the workforce can transition to new roles that complement AI.

While AI offers remarkable capabilities in data processing, pattern recognition, and predictive analytics, it is constrained by limitations in data dependency, emotional intelligence, creativity, ethical reasoning, and accountability. These limitations highlight the need for a balanced approach that integrates AI's strengths with human oversight and capabilities. By understanding and addressing these constraints, organizations can effectively harness AI to complement human skills and drive innovation while mitigating risks and ensuring ethical standards.

A critical analysis of AI's future capabilities highlights both promising advancements and significant challenges that lie ahead. AI is expected to continue its rapid development, enhancing its ability to process and analyze vast amounts of data with even greater speed and accuracy. Future AI systems are likely to become more sophisticated in pattern recognition, enabling more precise predictions and decision-making. These advancements could revolutionize industries such as healthcare, finance, and transportation by improving diagnostics, optimizing investment strategies, and enhancing autonomous vehicle performance.

However, as AI evolves, the issue of data dependency will remain crucial. While future AI may develop more advanced techniques for handling incomplete or biased data, the quality and integrity of the data it relies on will still be a fundamental concern. Efforts to improve data collection methods, ensure data diversity, and mitigate biases will be essential to fully realize AI's potential.

The future of AI also promises improvements in its capacity for emotional intelligence and human interaction. Advancements in natural language processing and machine learning could enable AI to better understand and respond to human emotions. This could enhance AI's effectiveness in customer service, therapy, and other fields requiring nuanced human interaction. Despite these advancements, AI will still struggle to genuinely empathize and form deep emotional connections, which are inherently human traits.

Creativity and innovation are areas where AI is expected to make strides, but significant limitations will persist. AI can assist in the creative process by generating ideas and suggesting solutions based on extensive data analysis. However, the ability to think outside the box and create truly novel concepts will remain challenging for AI. Human creativity, driven by intuition, personal experiences, and emotional depth, is unlikely to be fully replicated by AI.

Ethical and moral reasoning in AI will continue to be a critical area of development. Future AI systems may incorporate more sophisticated ethical frameworks and decision-making algorithms to better navigate complex moral dilemmas. Nonetheless, the absence of genuine moral understanding will necessitate ongoing human oversight to ensure that AI operates within acceptable ethical boundaries. Establishing robust guidelines and regulatory frameworks will be essential to manage AI's ethical implications effectively.

Accountability and transparency in AI will become increasingly important as AI systems take on more significant roles in decision-making. Future advancements may include more transparent AI models that provide clearer explanations for their decisions. This could help address concerns about accountability and build trust in AI systems. However, ensuring that AI decisions are fair, unbiased, and understandable to humans will remain a challenging task.

The potential impact of AI on employment and the economy is another area of critical importance. As AI systems become more advanced, they will likely automate a wider range of tasks, including those that currently require human cognitive skills. This could lead to significant job displacement across various industries. To mitigate these effects, there will be a growing need for strategies focused on reskilling and upskilling the workforce, preparing individuals for new roles that emerge alongside AI advancements. These strategies will be essential in ensuring that the benefits of AI do not come at the expense of widespread economic disruption and unemployment.

AI's role in augmenting human capabilities will expand. Instead of merely automating tasks, future AI systems will work more collaboratively with humans, enhancing their abilities and enabling them to achieve more complex and creative outcomes. This augmentation could revolutionize fields such as medicine, engineering, and the arts, where AI could provide new tools and insights that significantly enhance human performance. However, the integration of AI into society will continue to raise profound ethical and societal questions. Issues related to privacy, security, and the potential misuse of AI technologies will need ongoing attention. Ensuring that AI systems are designed and used in ways that respect individual rights and societal values will be a key challenge for policymakers, technologists, and ethicists.

The global landscape of AI development will also shape its future capabilities. Advances in AI will be influenced by the competitive dynamics between major technology hubs, such as the United States, China, and the European Union. These regions will play crucial roles in setting standards, driving innovation, and addressing the ethical and regulatory challenges associated with AI. International collaboration and dialogue will be necessary to establish common frameworks that ensure AI development benefits humanity as a whole. In conclusion, the future capabilities of AI promise significant advancements that could transform various aspects of society. However, these advancements come with challenges that must be carefully managed. Ensuring the quality and integrity of data, addressing the limitations of AI in emotional intelligence and creativity, navigating ethical and moral dilemmas, and managing the socio-economic impacts will be critical. By addressing these challenges, society can harness the full potential of AI while mitigating its risks, ultimately leading to a more innovative, efficient, and equitable world.

Implementing AI-driven leadership involves a range of technical, operational, and social challenges, as well as potential risks and unintended consequences. Successfully navigating these complexities is essential for organizations looking to leverage AI's capabilities in leadership roles. Technical and operational challenges of implementing AI-driven leadership are significant. Developing and deploying AI systems that are reliable, secure, and capable of performing leadership tasks require substantial technical expertise and resources. One major challenge is ensuring the quality and accuracy of the data used to train AI models. Poor-quality or biased data can lead to flawed decision-making, which can have serious repercussions for an organization. Additionally, integrating AI systems with existing infrastructure and processes can be complex and costly. Ensuring interoperability and seamless communication between AI and other business systems is crucial for operational efficiency.

Another technical challenge is maintaining the security and robustness of AI systems. AI-driven leadership systems must be resilient against cyberattacks and data breaches, which requires ongoing investment in cybersecurity measures. Moreover, continuous monitoring and updating of AI systems are necessary to ensure they adapt to changing environments and emerging threats. Operationally, organizations must also consider the scalability of AI solutions, ensuring they can handle increased workloads and expand as the organization grows.

Resistance to AI from employees and stakeholders poses a significant challenge. Many employees may fear that AI will replace their jobs, leading to job insecurity and resistance to AI initiatives. This resistance can hinder the successful implementation of AI systems and reduce their effectiveness. Similarly, stakeholders, including customers, partners, and regulators, may have concerns about the ethical implications, transparency, and accountability of AI-driven leadership. Addressing these concerns through clear communication, transparency, and engagement is essential to build trust and acceptance.

Managing the transition to AI-driven leadership requires careful planning and change management strategies. Organizations need to develop comprehensive transition plans that include reskilling and upskilling programs for employees, ensuring they are equipped to work alongside AI technologies and take on new roles that AI cannot perform. Effective communication is critical to alleviate fears and highlight the benefits of AI integration, such as increased efficiency, better decision-making, and new opportunities for growth.

Leaders should also foster a culture of innovation and continuous learning, encouraging employees to embrace new technologies and adapt to changing circumstances. Providing ongoing support and resources, such as training programs and access to learning platforms, can help employees develop the skills needed to thrive in an AI-augmented workplace. Additionally, involving employees in the AI implementation process by seeking their input and addressing their concerns can increase buy-in and reduce resistance.

Potential risks and unintended consequences of AI-driven leadership must be carefully considered. One significant risk is the potential for AI systems to make erroneous or biased decisions. If not properly managed, these decisions can lead to negative outcomes, such as discrimination, financial losses, or reputational damage. Ensuring robust oversight and implementing checks and balances are crucial to mitigate these risks. Organizations should establish clear governance frameworks that define the roles and responsibilities of human oversight, ensuring that AI systems operate within ethical and legal boundaries.

Another risk is the over-reliance on AI, which can lead to the erosion of critical human skills, such as judgment, empathy, and creativity. While AI can enhance decision-making, it cannot replicate the nuanced understanding and emotional intelligence that human leaders bring. Ensuring a balanced approach, where AI complements rather than replaces human capabilities, is essential to maintaining effective leadership. The displacement of jobs due to AI automation can have broader societal implications, such as increased unemployment and economic inequality. Addressing these issues requires coordinated efforts between businesses, governments, and educational institutions to create policies and programs that support workforce transition and social safety nets.

The future of AI-driven leadership is poised for significant evolution as technology continues to advance and organizations increasingly integrate AI into their operations. Predictions for the evolution of AI-driven leadership suggest a shift towards more sophisticated and autonomous AI systems that can handle complex decision-making processes, enhance strategic planning, and optimize operational efficiency. As AI technologies become more advanced, we can expect them to play a more central role in leadership, complementing and augmenting human capabilities in unprecedented ways.

Predictions for the evolution of AI-driven leadership include the development of AI systems that can provide real-time, data-driven insights across all aspects of business operations. These systems will not only analyze past and present data but also predict future trends with greater accuracy, enabling leaders to make proactive and informed decisions. AI-driven leadership will likely become more personalized, with AI tailoring its recommendations and actions based on the unique needs and preferences of individual leaders and organizations.

Emerging technologies that could further enhance or challenge AI's role in leadership encompass a broad range of innovations. Quantum computing, for example, holds the potential to exponentially increase the processing power of AI systems, allowing for more complex analyses and faster decision-making. This could enable AI to solve problems and optimize processes that are currently beyond its capabilities. Additionally, advancements in natural language processing (NLP) and emotional AI could improve AI's ability to understand and respond to human emotions and language nuances, making AI-driven leadership more empathetic and effective in human interactions. However, these advancements also pose challenges. The integration of these emerging technologies will require significant investment and technical expertise, and organizations will need to navigate the ethical and legal implications of more powerful and autonomous AI systems. Ensuring that these systems are transparent, fair, and accountable will be crucial to maintaining trust and preventing misuse.

Long-term implications for organizational structures and leadership models will be profound as AI-driven leadership becomes more prevalent. Traditional hierarchical structures may evolve into more dynamic and flexible models, with AI systems facilitating decentralized decision-making and empowering teams to operate with greater autonomy. This shift could lead to flatter organizational structures where leadership is distributed, and decision-making is more collaborative and data-driven.

AI-driven leadership will also necessitate new leadership models that prioritize continuous learning, adaptability, and innovation. Leaders will need to develop new skills to effectively collaborate with AI, including technical literacy, data interpretation, and ethical decision-making. Organizations will need to invest in leadership development programs that equip current and future leaders with these skills, ensuring they can navigate the complexities of an AI-augmented workplace.

The integration of AI into leadership roles will impact corporate culture. Organizations will need to foster a culture that embraces technology while maintaining a strong focus on human values and relationships. Balancing the efficiency and data-driven capabilities of AI with the empathy, creativity, and ethical reasoning of human leaders will be essential to creating a harmonious and effective organizational environment.

In the long term, the widespread adoption of AI-driven leadership could lead to more efficient and innovative organizations capable of rapidly adapting to changing market conditions and technological advancements. However, this transition will also require careful management of the social and economic impacts, including job displacement and the need for reskilling and upskilling the workforce. The future outlook for AI-driven leadership is marked by significant opportunities and challenges. The evolution of AI technologies will enhance leadership capabilities, enabling more informed and proactive decision-making. Emerging technologies like quantum computing and emotional AI will further expand the potential of AI-driven leadership, while also posing new ethical and technical challenges. The long-term implications for organizational structures and leadership models will be transformative, requiring a balanced approach that leverages AI's strengths while preserving the essential qualities of human leadership. By navigating these changes thoughtfully and proactively, organizations can harness the power of AI to drive innovation, efficiency, and sustainable growth.

Conclusion

Our book has embarked on a comprehensive exploration of AI's transformative impact on leadership, illustrating how advanced technologies are reshaping the way leaders operate and make decisions. Throughout the chapters, we have delved into the fundamental concepts of AI, its applications across various industries, and the profound implications these technologies bring to the realm of leadership.

The journey began with a thorough examination of AI's fundamental concepts, including machine learning, natural language processing, and neural networks. These technologies form the backbone of modern AI systems, enabling them to analyze vast amounts of data, recognize patterns, and make predictions with remarkable accuracy. By understanding these foundational elements, we set the stage for exploring how AI can enhance and augment leadership functions.

AI's potential to revolutionize leadership is vast. From improving decision-making processes with data-driven insights to automating routine tasks and optimizing operations, AI offers leaders unprecedented tools to increase efficiency and effectiveness. The integration of AI into leadership roles allows for more strategic planning, proactive management, and innovative problem-solving, ultimately driving organizational success and competitiveness.

We explored the implications of AI across different sectors, highlighting how industries such as healthcare, finance, retail, and transportation are being transformed by AI technologies. In healthcare, AI assists in diagnostics, personalized medicine, and predictive analytics, leading to better patient outcomes and more efficient resource management. In finance, AI enhances fraud detection, risk management, and automated trading, providing greater accuracy and speed in financial operations. Retailers leverage AI for personalized recommendations, inventory management, and customer service, improving the overall shopping experience and operational efficiency. In transportation, AI drives advancements in autonomous vehicles, traffic management, and logistics optimization, contributing to safer and more efficient travel and delivery systems.

These industry-specific applications demonstrate the versatility and power of AI, reinforcing the importance of leaders understanding and harnessing these technologies to stay ahead in their respective fields. The ability to leverage AI effectively can provide a significant competitive advantage, enabling organizations to innovate and adapt in an ever-changing landscape.

The integration of AI is not without its challenges. Ethical and social considerations are paramount in ensuring that AI technologies are used responsibly and align with societal values. The book addressed critical issues such as data privacy, algorithmic bias, and the potential for job displacement. Ensuring transparency, accountability, and fairness in AI-driven decisions is essential to maintaining trust and credibility.

Leaders must navigate these ethical challenges by establishing robust governance frameworks and ethical guidelines for AI deployment. This includes regular audits of AI systems for bias, implementing secure data practices, and promoting transparency in AI decision-making processes. Additionally, the social implications of AI, particularly regarding employment and workforce dynamics, require thoughtful strategies for reskilling and upskilling employees to prepare them for an AI-augmented future.

As AI technologies become increasingly integral to business operations, the need for evolving leadership models is more critical than ever. Traditional leadership approaches must be redefined to meet the demands of a rapidly changing technological landscape. This involves developing adaptive, agile, and innovative leadership models that can effectively leverage AI while maintaining the essential qualities of human leadership.

The pace of technological advancement and market dynamics necessitates that leaders be more flexible and responsive. Adaptive leadership involves being open to change and able to pivot strategies quickly in response to new information or shifts in the business environment. This agility allows leaders to seize new opportunities and mitigate risks effectively. Innovative leadership, on the other hand, emphasizes the importance of fostering creativity and encouraging experimentation. Leaders must be willing to challenge the status quo and explore novel solutions to complex problems, harnessing AI's capabilities to drive innovation.

A key aspect of evolving leadership models is the integration of AI-driven insights. AI provides leaders with powerful tools to analyze data, predict trends, and make evidence-based decisions. However, it is crucial to balance these capabilities with human intuition, creativity, and emotional intelligence. AI can handle routine tasks and data-intensive processes, freeing leaders to focus on strategic thinking and human-centric responsibilities. For instance, while AI might analyze market trends and suggest strategic directions, human leaders are needed to interpret these insights within the broader context of organizational goals and values, and to inspire and motivate their teams to execute these strategies effectively.

Successful integration of AI into leadership involves using AI for data analysis and operational efficiencies while relying on human judgment for strategic and ethical decision-making. Ensuring that AI systems are transparent and their decision-making processes can be explained and scrutinized is essential. Maintaining a human-centric approach to leadership, where empathy, ethical reasoning, and relationship-building are prioritized, is also crucial.

To thrive in the AI era, leaders must cultivate a growth mindset—an openness to learning, adapting, and continuously improving. This mindset enables leaders to embrace new technologies, learn from failures, and encourage innovation within their teams. A growth mindset fosters resilience and agility, qualities essential for navigating the uncertainties of an AI-driven world. Creating a culture ready for AI integration involves promoting continuous learning and development. Leaders should provide opportunities for their teams to upskill and reskill, ensuring they are equipped to work alongside AI technologies. Encouraging experimentation and risk-taking is also vital. A culture that values innovation allows employees to explore new ideas without fear of failure. This can lead to breakthrough innovations and improvements. Transparent communication about the advantages of AI and addressing fears related to job displacement or privacy concerns can help build trust and buy-in from employees.

The evolving landscape of AI requires a fundamental shift in leadership models. Leaders must be adaptive, agile, and innovative, integrating AI-driven insights while maintaining the human qualities essential for effective leadership. By cultivating a growth mindset and fostering a culture ready for AI integration, leaders can navigate the complexities of the AI era, driving their organizations toward sustainable success and innovation.

Ethical considerations and governance are critical when integrating AI into leadership roles. Emphasizing transparency, accountability, and the mitigation of biases in AI systems is paramount to ensuring that these technologies are used responsibly and fairly. Transparency in AI decision-making means making the processes and logic behind AI systems clear and understandable to all stakeholders. This openness helps build trust, as stakeholders can see how decisions are made and verify that they align with ethical standards and organizational values. Accountability involves establishing clear lines of responsibility for AI decisions, ensuring that there is always a human oversight mechanism in place to address any issues that arise.

Mitigating biases in AI systems is another essential aspect of ethical governance. AI systems can unintentionally perpetuate and even amplify existing biases present in the data they are trained on. To counteract this, it is crucial to use diverse and representative datasets and continuously monitor AI outputs for signs of bias. Regular audits and updates to AI systems can help ensure they remain fair and impartial. In addition, involving diverse teams in the development and deployment of AI can provide multiple perspectives and help identify and mitigate potential biases.

The necessity of ethical and legal frameworks cannot be overstated. These frameworks are essential for maintaining trust in AI-driven decisions. Ethical frameworks should include guidelines for data privacy, ensuring that personal information is collected and used responsibly. They should also outline procedures for addressing ethical dilemmas and ensuring that AI systems operate within the bounds of accepted moral and societal standards. Legal frameworks, meanwhile, provide the regulatory backbone needed to enforce these ethical guidelines. Compliance with regulations such as the General Data Protection Regulation (GDPR) and the California Consumer Privacy Act (CCPA) is crucial for protecting individual privacy and maintaining public trust.

Legal frameworks should be adaptive, keeping pace with the rapid development of AI technologies. They need to address new challenges as they arise, such as the potential for AI to make decisions that have significant impacts on people's lives. This includes establishing protocols for transparency in AI algorithms, mandating regular impact assessments, and creating avenues for redress when AI decisions lead to adverse outcomes.

The future capabilities of AI hold tremendous potential for enhancing productivity and decision-making across various sectors. As AI technologies continue to evolve, they will increasingly automate routine tasks, analyze vast datasets, and provide sophisticated insights that can drive more informed and strategic decisions. AI's ability to process information at unprecedented speeds and recognize patterns that may be invisible to the human eye enables leaders to make decisions based on comprehensive data analysis, thereby improving efficiency and accuracy.

Despite these impressive capabilities, it is crucial to recognize the inherent limitations of AI. One of the most significant limitations is AI's inability to replicate human emotional intelligence, creativity, and ethical reasoning. Emotional intelligence involves understanding and managing one's own emotions, as well as recognizing and influencing the emotions of others. This quality is essential for effective leadership, particularly in building relationships, fostering teamwork, and resolving conflicts. AI, however advanced, lacks the capacity to genuinely empathize with human feelings and navigate the complexities of human interactions.

Similarly, creativity remains a distinctly human trait that AI struggles to emulate. While AI can assist in generating ideas by identifying patterns and suggesting possibilities based on existing data, it does not possess the intrinsic human ability to think outside the box, imagine novel solutions, or bring innovative concepts to fruition in the same way humans do. Creativity often stems from personal experiences, cultural contexts, and intuitive leaps that are beyond the reach of AI algorithms.

Ethical reasoning is another critical area where AI falls short. Making ethical decisions requires a deep understanding of moral principles, empathy, and the ability to weigh the broader implications of actions on society and individuals. AI can be programmed with ethical guidelines, but it lacks the nuanced judgment needed to navigate complex ethical dilemmas. For instance, deciding between competing ethical values or understanding the subtleties of human rights issues requires a level of moral discernment that AI cannot achieve.

The role of human qualities in effective leadership alongside AI is therefore indispensable. Leaders must leverage AI's analytical power and efficiency to enhance their decision-making processes, but they must also bring their uniquely human qualities to the forefront. Emotional intelligence allows leaders to connect with their teams on a personal level, building trust and fostering a positive work environment. Creativity enables leaders to innovate and drive progress, finding solutions that AI alone might not identify. Ethical reasoning ensures that decisions are made with a consideration of their broader impact, maintaining the integrity and social responsibility of the organization. The most effective leaders will be those who can integrate AI into their leadership practices while maintaining a strong human touch. This involves creating a collaborative environment where AI tools are used to augment human capabilities rather than replace them. By balancing AI's strengths with human intuition, empathy, and creativity, leaders can navigate the complexities of modern business landscapes more effectively.

The current state of AI and leadership is marked by significant advancements in technology and a growing recognition of AI's transformative potential. AI technologies have progressed rapidly, enabling unprecedented capabilities in data processing, machine learning, natural language processing, and predictive analytics. These advancements have opened up new possibilities for enhancing decision-making and operational efficiency across various industries.

AI's integration into industries such as healthcare, finance, retail, and transportation has already demonstrated its potential to revolutionize traditional business practices. In healthcare, AI systems analyze medical images for diagnostics, predict patient outcomes, and personalize treatment plans, leading to improved patient care and more efficient resource allocation. In finance, AI enhances fraud detection, automates trading, and optimizes risk management, providing a more robust and dynamic financial ecosystem. Retail businesses leverage AI for personalized marketing, inventory management, and customer service, significantly enhancing the customer experience and operational efficiency. In transportation, AI drives the development of autonomous vehicles, optimizes traffic management, and improves logistics, contributing to safer and more efficient travel and delivery systems.

Despite these advancements, integrating AI into leadership and business operations presents several challenges and limitations, particularly concerning data quality and ethical implications. High-quality, unbiased data is critical for the effective functioning of AI systems. However, data often contains biases or is incomplete, leading to skewed results and potentially unfair or inaccurate decision-making. Ensuring data integrity requires rigorous processes for data collection, cleaning, and validation. Additionally, AI systems must be regularly updated with new data to maintain their accuracy and relevance.

Ethical implications of AI integration are another major concern. AI systems can inadvertently perpetuate biases present in their training data, leading to discriminatory outcomes. For example, an AI system used for hiring might favor certain demographics over others if the historical hiring data it was trained on contains biases. Addressing these ethical challenges involves implementing robust oversight mechanisms, conducting regular audits, and developing AI systems with fairness and accountability in mind. Organizations must also establish clear ethical guidelines and governance frameworks to guide the responsible use of AI.

Transparency and accountability in AI decision-making are crucial for maintaining trust among stakeholders. AI systems should be designed to provide explanations for their decisions, enabling users to understand and challenge these outcomes if necessary. This transparency helps ensure that AI decisions are fair and justifiable. Moreover, accountability measures must be in place to address any negative consequences resulting from AI decisions, with clearly defined roles and responsibilities for managing and mitigating such outcomes.

The social implications of AI integration, particularly concerning employment, cannot be overlooked. While AI has the potential to enhance productivity and create new job opportunities, it also poses a risk of job displacement, especially for routine and repetitive tasks. Preparing the workforce for this transition involves investing in reskilling and upskilling programs to equip employees with the skills needed to thrive in an AI-augmented workplace. This proactive approach can help mitigate the adverse effects of job displacement and ensure a smoother transition to new roles that leverage human creativity, emotional intelligence, and strategic thinking.

Embracing AI responsibly involves maintaining ethical considerations at the forefront of AI integration. This means ensuring that AI systems are transparent, accountable, and fair. Addressing issues such as data bias, privacy, and the impact of AI on employment is essential to maintain trust and credibility. Ethical frameworks and robust governance structures must guide the development and deployment of AI technologies to align with societal values and benefit a broad range of stakeholders.

Promoting interdisciplinary teamwork is crucial for effectively leveraging both human and AI strengths. Combining diverse perspectives from various fields can enhance problem-solving and drive innovation. This collaborative approach ensures that AI is used to complement human capabilities rather than replace them, fostering a more inclusive and effective work environment.

Leaders must take proactive steps to shape AI's impact on their organizations and society. This includes fostering a culture of continuous learning, where employees are encouraged to develop new skills and stay updated on AI advancements. Encouraging innovation through experimentation and risk-taking helps organizations stay competitive and adapt to changing environments. Maintaining a strong ethical focus in AI integration is vital to address potential risks and ensure that AI technologies are used responsibly and align with organizational values and societal expectations.

The synergy of human and AI leadership is essential for effective leadership in the AI era. Collaboration and balance are key components in this dynamic, ensuring that AI technologies enhance rather than replace human potential. By working together, AI and human leaders can achieve more than either could alone, blending the analytical power of AI with the creativity, empathy, and ethical judgment that are uniquely human.

Ensuring that AI enhances human potential without replacing essential human qualities involves a thoughtful integration of technology into leadership practices. AI can handle data-intensive tasks, providing insights and recommendations that help leaders make more informed decisions. However, it is the human qualities of empathy, ethical reasoning, and creativity that drive innovation, build relationships, and inspire teams. Leaders must strike a balance, leveraging AI's strengths while preserving these critical human attributes. This balance allows for a leadership model that is both efficient and humane, capable of navigating complex interpersonal dynamics and ethical dilemmas.

Visionary leadership plays a crucial role in guiding organizations through AI integration and its complexities. Visionary leaders understand the potential of AI and are proactive in exploring its applications while being mindful of its limitations and ethical implications. They set a clear vision for how AI will be integrated into their organizations, aligning technological advancements with the organization's values and goals. These leaders foster a culture of innovation and continuous learning, encouraging their teams to embrace AI as a tool for growth and improvement.

By maintaining a focus on human-centric leadership and ethical AI use, visionary leaders ensure that the integration of AI technologies is conducted responsibly. They prioritize transparency and accountability, making sure that AI systems are understandable and their impacts are monitored and managed. This approach builds trust within the organization and with external stakeholders, ensuring that AI-driven decisions are fair and just.

The relationship between AI and leadership is multifaceted, reflecting both the transformative potential of AI and the enduring importance of human qualities in leadership. Throughout this book, we have explored how AI can revolutionize leadership practices, offering powerful tools for data analysis, decision-making, and operational efficiency. AI's capabilities enable leaders to access unprecedented insights, predict trends, and make more informed decisions, ultimately enhancing productivity and driving innovation.

While the potential of AI to transform leadership practices is immense, it is crucial to emphasize the irreplaceable human qualities that remain at the heart of effective leadership. Empathy, ethical reasoning, creativity, and emotional intelligence are qualities that AI cannot replicate. These attributes are essential for building relationships, fostering collaboration, and navigating complex interpersonal dynamics. Leaders must ensure that AI complements rather than replaces these human qualities, leveraging technology to enhance their capabilities while maintaining a human-centric approach.

To embrace AI responsibly and effectively, leaders should adhere to several key recommendations. First, they must maintain ethical considerations at the forefront of AI integration, ensuring transparency, accountability, and fairness in AI-driven decisions. Establishing robust ethical frameworks and governance structures is vital for guiding the responsible use of AI and aligning it with organizational values and societal expectations.

Promoting interdisciplinary teamwork is essential for leveraging both human and AI strengths. By combining diverse perspectives, organizations can enhance problem-solving and drive innovation. This collaborative approach ensures that AI is used to complement human capabilities, fostering a more inclusive and effective work environment.

Leaders should take proactive steps to shape AI's impact on their organizations and society. Fostering a culture of continuous learning is crucial, encouraging employees to develop new skills and stay updated on AI advancements. Encouraging innovation through experimentation and risk-taking helps organizations stay competitive and adapt to changing environments.

Visionary leadership is critical for guiding organizations through the complexities of AI integration. Visionary leaders set a clear vision for how AI will be integrated into their organizations, aligning technological advancements with the organization's values and goals. They prioritize transparency and accountability, ensuring that AI systems are understandable and their impacts are monitored and managed.

Throughout this book, we have delved into the multifaceted relationship between AI and leadership, examining how AI can revolutionize leadership practices while highlighting the enduring importance of human qualities. AI offers powerful tools for data analysis, decision-making, and operational efficiency, enabling leaders to access unprecedented insights, predict trends, and make more informed decisions. The potential of AI to transform leadership practices is immense, enhancing productivity and driving innovation across various industries.

It is crucial to remember that the most effective leadership combines the strengths of AI with the irreplaceable human qualities of empathy, ethical reasoning, creativity, and emotional intelligence. These attributes are essential for building relationships, fostering collaboration, and navigating complex interpersonal dynamics. Leaders must ensure that AI complements rather than replaces these human qualities, leveraging technology to enhance their capabilities while maintaining a human-centric approach.

To embrace AI responsibly and effectively, leaders must maintain ethical considerations at the forefront of AI integration, ensuring transparency, accountability, and fairness in AI-driven decisions. Establishing robust ethical frameworks and governance structures is vital for guiding the responsible use of AI and aligning it with organizational values and societal expectations. Promoting interdisciplinary teamwork is essential for leveraging both human and AI strengths, enhancing problem-solving, and driving innovation. Leaders should take proactive steps to shape AI's impact on their organizations and society by fostering a culture of continuous learning and encouraging innovation through experimentation and risk-taking. Visionary leadership is critical for guiding organizations through the complexities of AI integration, setting a clear vision for how AI will be incorporated, and prioritizing transparency and accountability.

As we navigate the AI landscape, thoughtful and visionary leadership will be essential. Leaders must balance technological advancements with the human touch, ensuring that AI enhances human potential without overshadowing it. By creating a future where technology and humanity thrive together, we can achieve a harmonious and effective leadership model that drives sustainable success and positive societal impact. This balanced integration of AI and human qualities will enable organizations to harness the transformative power of AI while maintaining the values and ethical standards that are crucial for long-term success. As we look ahead, the collaboration between human intuition and AI's analytical power will guide us through the complexities of a rapidly evolving technological landscape, fostering a more inclusive, innovative, and ethical world.

www.ingramcontent.com/pod-product-compliance
Lightning Source LLC
Chambersburg PA
CBHW050213230526
45470CB00001B/362